The Body Language
of Dance

The Body Language of Dance

Enhancing Your Dance Experience Through Its Spiritual Aspects

CARLOS GUTIÉRREZ

Library of Congress Number: 2001117431
ISBN #:   Hardcover   1-4010-1460-7
                    Softcover   1-4010-1461-5

Names, characters, places and incidents are the product of the author's
imagination and any resemblance to any actual persons, living or dead,
events, or locales is entirely coincidental.

Cover Photographs by Xenophon G. Stamoulis
This book was printed in the United States of America.

To order additional copies of this book,
contact:
Xlibris Corporation
1-888-795-4274
www.Xlibris.com
Orders@Xlibris.com

Contents

PART V

BODY LANGUAGE ON THE DANCE FLOOR

PART VI

BRAIN DOMINANCE

PART VII

APPENDIX

Acknowledgements

I would like to thank all of my dance part-
ners, friends and students who contributed,
both directly and indirectly, to make this book possible: Glynis
Alder, Ira Hamburg, Betty Kester Lezzana, Judy Hamburg,
Lauren Rubenstein, Stephanie Richardson, Jeannine Mantz, and
Diane Taylor. Special thanks to my dance partner and editor
Kathryn Abdul-Baki and to my friend and student Joyce Briggs
for putting this book together.

A special thanks to my parents, Victor and Josefa Gutierrez
for their artistic and spiritual influence. As always, my love
and thanks to my wife and dance partner Nicole and our two
daughters Celina Angelica and Rafaela Adriana for their love,
support, and inspiration.

Note: I have purposely avoided using the words 'better' and 'worse' since I believe that a thing or person is not better or worse than another, but only different and special. 'Better' and 'worse' tend to lead to judgments and put downs of the self and others. Moreover, the word *better* gives an impression of superiority while *worse* gives an impression of inferiority. We are all one, equal, and different.

Author's Note

In the last 15 years ballroom dancing has become another big industry in society as a way to express oneself and develop physical, mental and spiritual fitness. In the last two decades new information has come to me through you about your dance body language, your body shapes, and your right and left brain characteristics.

Everything begins with your perception and awareness about yourself (life), and how you create everything that is happening to you, such as attracting a particular partner or instructor who can help you become aware of who you really are. In addition, breaking away from your old value system and society's restrictions can also help your dancing by enabling you to be more yourself.

Whether you consider it a sport, recreation, an art or a mode of emotional or physical expression, ballroom dancing is becoming more popular each day. Dancing can bring out your soul and for some, can be an almost mystical experience. In other words, music wakes up the soul and the body responds naturally.

Over the past fifteen years, more and more men and women have begun taking ballroom dance lessons. Many students or prospective students want guidance on getting the most out of instruction and practice. Students and instructors alike want help with interacting with each other or with a partner. In this millennium, people are concerned about what they communicate through their body language while dancing, what their body features say to others, and how they unconsciously reveal their right and left-brain personalities with different partners. If you have any of these interests or concerns, this book is for you.

A dancing figure is a very powerful figure. It is direct and forceful. It comes from the side of dreams and desires, the underside and inside of our most primitive and real selves. It is sensual and sexual and romantic and yearning. Our masks are exposed. Many people for this reason won't dance.

A former student.

How This Book Came to Be

To give you some background on how this book came to be, I need to tell you about myself. I am the fourth child of six, born in Matucana, Peru, in 1955. I was 6 years old when I began to speak for the first time, because I unconsciously shut out the outside world in order to be aware of my own inner world. Even as a young child I was aware of my spirituality and perceived thoughts and intentions from people. I was also aware of seeing energy or auras. When I was 8 years old I naturally understood about eternal life or reincarnation, I also sensed that this was leading me to become a teacher or spiritual counselor. Indeed, throughout my life I have always had people coming to me with their personal problems searching for advice.

I come from an artistic and spiritual family—my father was an amateur bullfighter, a talented singer in Peru, and an accomplished art restorer at the Metropolitan Museum of Art in New York. He also has a gift of knowing people very well after the first or second meeting. My two sisters, Ledda and Patricia Roxana were also talented singers, and my brother Jimmy is a professional artist and a Tango dance instructor. My mother on the other hand, has always been interested in the use of natural herbs for healing, and as a creative seamstress, has been making many of my dance outfits for my professional dancing. She also has a highly developed intuition and spirituality. It seemed perfectly natural, therefore, that my own professional career would ultimately combine both the artistic and spiritual elements to which I had been exposed all my life. For as well as my love for dance I have been a professional artist, and a spiritual Reiki healer and teacher for 20 years. I also give lectures about metaphysical psychology and spirituality.

Soon after my arrival in the United States in 1977, I decided to become a hustle dance instructor, since that was the most popular dance at the time. Later, I became a ballroom dance instructor for three major dance studios in the Washington DC area. In the twenty five years that I have taught dancing, I have had the opportunity to interact closely with many of my students. I enjoy being around dancers, and teaching allows me to know and understand myself and others more effectively.

Even before I began teaching dancing, I was very sociable and sought the company of others. From a very young age, I found myself observing people's body features and body language very closely. Over the years I have become increasingly aware of the meaning behind certain gestures and looks, not only from observing others but also from observing myself. I noticed, for example, that most parts of the left side of my body are slightly bigger, stronger, and heavier than my right side. My left leg for instance, is bigger than the right, and I have stronger vision in my left eye. I have smaller than normal wrists, and a protruding rib-cage, deep-set eyes, and very little hair on my body. These are just some of my physical characteristics, which I later intuitively understood before observing and understanding others.

Soon I began wondering about dancers and all their habitual non-verbal gestures, looks and movements. At first, my observations were nothing more than the result of healthy curiosity. Then, after years of close interaction with dancers of all ages and nationalities, including the blind, the physically and mentally challenged, and those with polio, I realized that dancing was bringing me closer to the inner world of my students as well as my own. Therefore, I believe that everyone I encounter in my life has contributed to this book by making me aware of something deeper about the psychology of dancing than merely social skills and communication.

I began to systematize what I was learning and was most fortunate that, throughout my research, many of my students cooperated by responding to my many probing questions. Those responses validated my intuitive observations. After more than two decades of research, although I had never consciously thought to write a book, I concluded that I should share my observations and experiences by writing about them for you.

Very little has been written to help trained dancers as well as street dancers, and students and instructors of ballroom dancing from the emotional or psychological aspect. Most literature in the field describes steps rather than providing the practical information and the support for decision-making that can make or break the dance learning experience. This book gives you that information.

Although books have been written over the years about "body language," nothing has been written about the *spiritual* body language of dance. This book can help you to read and understand your own dance body language and physical characteristics: Why for example, some dancers keep their fingers pointed up in the air while holding the hand of their partners during a dance. Why some pull their partners close. Why some dancers are pigeon-toed. Why one side of a person's body is bigger and stronger than the other side.

You can use this book to move into the 21st century of awareness as you learn to spiritually interact more effectively with one another: Students and instructors can learn to interact with different partners or instructors and build self-confidence through dancing.

This unconventional approach to the psychology of dancers may make you more aware of your own behavior on and off the dance floor. While conventional instructors teach steps, techniques, and styles, I have found the greatest beauty and joy in watching my students discover their inner selves as they learn. My way of teaching is to bring out your confidence and awareness of who you are in the process, and help you to understand that you may not need many restrictions, intimidation, or fear of criticism to do steps correctly. I believe that you can learn to dance more quickly when you are relaxed and happy and retain a sense of humor throughout this wonderful process.

How This Book Is Organized

This book contains an introduction, two major sections each with several chapters, and an appendix:

- Part I describes the benefits of ballroom dancing as well as the links between your thoughts, your emotions, and your behavior.
- Part II contains chapters to help you prepare and train to be a ballroom dancer. With this information, you can get the most benefit and joy from your lessons. This section provides a survey of the types of instruction available, including the characteristics of the best instructors, and contains guidelines for choosing an instructor. It also discusses expenses, and tells what to expect from your lessons.
- Part III contains information to help you as you apply what you are learning. It provides alternative approaches to learning and practice, discusses how to handle various situations that may arise in the dance setting, dance floor etiquette, the search for a regular partner, and ways to

take care of yourself. It also provides some sources of inspiration and ways to restore peace of mind during your dance education.

- Part IV offers suggestions for competitors or those who are considering competing. It explains the advantages and disadvantages of dance competitions, and provides help in areas such as choosing the environment, what to wear, what to expect, and the impact of tension and stress. Finally, there are guidelines for deciding whether to become a professional dancer.

- Part V contains reference material to help you analyze yourself and others as you continue your ballroom dancing experience. This information can help you understand yourself, your actions, and the attitudes you exhibit on the dance floor, regardless of where you learned to dance. This information can lead to self-knowledge and provide you with a different understanding of your partners, so you can interact more successfully with them. There is a chapter on the physical features of the face and body as indicators of personality or emotional state. There is also a chapter that describes the facets of self-presentation, including posture, gestures and conscious facial expressions, and partnering styles, along with their implications.

- Part VI discusses the behaviors that are indicators of right or left-brain dominance. It also discusses the impact of the dominant hemisphere in the dance setting.

- Part VII (the appendix) contains a brief history of ballroom dances, types of music, lyrics and their impact, and a final word.

PART I
INTRODUCTION

The more evolved you become, the more there is to know.

***

The more you love your job, the more you can help others.

***

Whatever you give away always comes back to you.

***

Optimism is the key to finding solutions for everything.

***

If the truth hurts, it is because it is true.

***

1

Chapter 1 What Ballroom Dancing Can Do for You

There are a number of motives for taking dance lessons, and ballroom dancing has distinct benefits.

Motives for Taking Dancing Lessons

- Learn to dance.
- Alleviate stress.
- Escape personal problems.
- Find romance.
- Love of music.
- Lose weight.
- Develop muscle coordination.
- Develop social skills.
- Develop self-confidence.
- Give a gift to yourself.
- Have a mode of self-expression.
- Have a way to meet others.
- Improve mental fitness.
- Improve physical fitness.

- Improve self awareness.
- Improve spiritual awareness.

Benefits of Ballroom Dancing

Ballroom dancing or partner dancing is easy to learn, and the advantages are many. In the process of learning to dance, men and women have often increased their self-esteem, their mental and physical health, and their spiritual awareness.

A Social Outlet and Source of Fun

Dancing can be your most sociable activity because it is fun. You will also meet people you would not have met in other settings. The dance setting promotes easy conversation and plenty to talk about, whether or not you know each other. Knowing how to dance gives you something to do with your leisure time and an activity to suggest to friends, family or dates.

Physical and Mental Benefits

Practicing dancing for a few hours a week can help you become healthier. Getting this regular exercise increases the amount of oxygen in your body, which leads to more physical energy and greater intellectual productivity. Dance movements produce a natural high, which can make you feel good about yourself. Leading and following, and moving through the steps, promotes endurance, improves your strength and muscle co-ordination, tunes your reflexes, and enables you to sleep more peacefully.

Emotional and Psychological Benefits

Dance movements stimulate a positive frame of mind and provide an outlet for emotions. Dancing is also a most pleasurable way of attaining joy and self-esteem. While dancing, you can set aside problems and alleviate stress. This "vacation" can enable you to return to the other details of your life more relaxed, and diminish angry behavior and uncertainties, while replacing them with a positive and constructive attitude. In turn, the more you dance, the more pleasure you can give to yourself and others.

Understanding the body language of dance enables you to know yourself and others more effectively. As you do so, your level of confidence and your ability to relate to others increases.

A Showcase for Your Gifts

Dancing provides you with a mode of artistic expression in which you can respond to the rhythm and melody of the music. It can enable you to exhibit your individual talents, and your communication skills. Dancing may also be the key to tapping your unrealized potentials. You may find that you have a passion for dance—and without realizing one's passion for something, one cannot truly have lived.

A Means for Making Changes in Your Life

Besides bringing harmony and enjoyment to your personal life, learning leading and following skills and practicing these skills can promote assertiveness, cooperation, and a more effective relationship with your partner and others. Lessons you learn in this regard will carry over to your other relationships.

Dancing can provide pleasure and replace the need for alcohol, drugs, and cigarettes. As said earlier, Ballroom dancing creates a natural high that enhances enjoyment of the power of the present moment and contributes to a healthier life. Therefore, as a successful, honest, happy dancer, you can live life one day at a time and be in the "now." By putting your positive thoughts into action today you can help heal negative experiences from your past.

Spiritual Benefits

Today's society still focuses mainly on the functions of the left-brain characteristics, providing very little opportunity for understanding the spiritual purpose of life. Ballroom dancing may provide that opportunity through self-expression. If you want to know what your soul desires, you must be in touch with your feelings of your present moment and thus become aware of what you most enjoy doing in life. Through dance, you can get in touch with your soul and with nature. You can experience the element of life that creates harmony and expresses beauty. You can choose a life that you love (such as that of a dancer) and you can enjoy yourself thoroughly. If you choose a living instead (not liking what you do, but making money), you may find your life filled with stress and resentment. This is because listening only to your mind (ego) may bring restrictions and many problems into your life.

Spirituality is the essence of life. It unites, loves, shares, protects, and accepts others for who they are. A lack of spirituality can lead you into chaos, ignorance, greed, suffering, selfishness, anger, violence, and pain. Spirituality helps you remember who you are:

- You are a soul with a body (your soul is God): Listening to your feelings or your heart of the present moment can help you make wiser decisions regarding yourself, others, and your dance community. You are not your past, you are only your now.

- We are all One: This can bring you closer together and help you develop more compassion and unity towards others. Whatever you do for yourself do for others, and whatever you do for others, do for yourself.
- The Meaning of life: You are not here to learn anything, only to remember who you are and experience what your soul already knows. Your soul, or God, communicates with you through feelings, inner voice or intuition, which helps you create anything you want to be or have in your life.
- There are no accidents or coincidences, nor victims or villains in life. Everything that is happening is happening because you and others are unconsciously or consciously creating them. If you want to change what you do not like, change your thoughts or perception about it.
- Your nature is to help yourself and others in time of confusion, need, injury, and sorrow because you are unconditionally loving.

Making decisions with your feelings may bring unity and happiness. Making decisions with your mind may bring chaos and conditional love. Making decisions with your emotions or past experiences may hold you back from becoming more of your true self.

PART II
PREPARING FOR YOUR DANCE EXPERIENCE

*It is not important how long a relationship lasts,
it is important that you are being yourself.*
***

*The more pleasure you give to yourself,
the more pleasure you can give to others.*
***

Dancing produces a natural high.
***

Laughing heals the body.
***

Like attracts like.
***

2

Chapter 2 Choosing a Way to Learn

Choosing the right setting for instruction and a good teacher can help you learn well and quickly.

Your Best Learning Situation

Begin with what you know best—yourself. What is the way you learn most successfully? What kind of person are you? If you have been dancing, what kind of dancer are you? Different dance studios offer dance instruction. This section deals with settings and the individuals who teach there. You need to find out about your instructor's background and experience before taking private lessons.

Type of Instruction and Instructional Setting

A number of settings exist for learning ballroom dancing. You may find that one of the following works differently for you than the others:

- Private instruction.
- Group classes.

- Workshops.
- Dance videos.
- Dance books.

Private Instruction

To find the most suitable setting for you, observe different studios with different instructors.

Private instruction can be scheduled at intervals that you work out with your instructor. The typical charge is $50–$95 an hour for a private lesson, depending on the instructor's experience. The setting for that instruction may vary, from a private home to a studio or other environment. Be alert to the following:

Distractions: In some settings, you may find yourself sharing the same room with other students and their instructors. This can be uncomfortable for you.

- If everyone is not learning the same dance, it is difficult to concentrate.
- If you are a natural dancer or a feeling dancer, you may tend to be more distracted by the music other instructors are playing. For example, if you are learning the Fox-trot but the other instructor is playing Mambo, you might start moving to the Mambo beat.
- If your instructor speaks loudly while teaching you, it can be disturbing to other instructors and students in the same room. It is important that everyone in the room, students and instructors alike, be comfortable during the lessons to make the time more productive. Therefore, if you do not like sharing the space during your private lesson, you must speak up and request a more private place or different time so you can get your money's worth. Taking a lesson during the day may be easier for you because there are not too many people in the studio.

- Your instructor should always have ready a selection of appropriate music for your dance lesson in order not to waste lesson time.
- Also, learning too many steps too fast because you want to get the most out of time may cause you to have difficulty remembering what you learned earlier, because you did not give yourself enough time to really pay attention to what you learned. On the other hand, learning your steps slowly without too much music can help you to retain and remember your steps, because they become more deeply imprinted in your muscle memory.

Interruptions: There are times when a private lesson is interrupted:

- If the phone rings and your instructor answers the call while you are concentrating and learning the steps of a dance, you may feel that the phone call is more important than your private lesson.
- If your instructor goes to the bathroom more than twice during your lesson, this can also be considered an interruption. You should have all of the instructor's attention.
- If the instructor does not face you while explaining the steps, perhaps he/she does not feel very involved with you or perhaps the instructor is feeling tired or stressed and thus is avoiding interaction with you. If this happens once or twice, you yourself may want to interrupt your lesson and reschedule. If it seems to be a pattern, you should consider a different time or day for the lessons or a different instructor.

Private Lessons at a Major Dance Studio

An instructor at a major dance studio may not be able to individualize the lessons for you:

- Each dance studio has its unique dance style and technique that you can learn. However, you and other students may look so much alike because all of you are learning the same style and technique that it may become boring. Studios should encourage you to add your own signature or style, so you can express your individuality.
- Some dance studios have policies that create separation and frustration among students and instructors. For example, some studios do not like you to take lessons from other studios or instructors, because they are afraid of losing money or students. Moreover, your instructors may not be permitted to teach you outside the studio because they can be fired. These restrictions prevent you and instructors from improving your dance skills in different settings.
- Beginner students can also be confused by taking dance lessons from many different instructors. All instructors teach differently according to their experiences and perceptions. Therefore, it is probably best to have one instructor until you become an intermediate level student before you choose to work with someone else.

Group Classes

Group classes are usually offered on a schedule that meets at regular intervals at a studio or nightclub. Seldom are they given in the instructor's home, due to space limitations. The length of the lesson (usually an hour), the curriculum, and the class schedule are set by the studio or instructor. Group classes are a good way to meet others who are interested in dancing and perhaps find a partner to practice with. Be aware of the following:

- The pace of the class may be too fast or too slow for your individual needs.
- The length of the lessons, or the intervals between lessons, may not be right for your learning style.
- Classes without music can be boring for you or can try your patience if you are a feeling dancer, since it is the music that inspires you.
- The class may not be evenly divided between men and women, so you may not always have a partner.

If you are an intermediate level dancer, it is important that you also practice with those who are beginners, because it can help you improve your lead. However, beginners can learn dancing faster during a group class by practicing with those intermediate level dancers who can help them remember the steps.

Dance Workshops

Workshops may be scheduled for a day, a weekend or longer. There are even dance camps you can attend. Be aware of the following:

- Dance workshops are enjoyable if you like to learn in large groups, meet people or dance with different partners. Many dance instructors charge from $30 to $40 for a dance workshop.
- Overbooking too many beginner students in a two-hour dance workshop can make it difficult to learn. If there are more than 40 students in the class with only one or two instructors, it can be a waste of time, or you may be neglected because there is not enough time to help everybody. Only people who have some experience may learn something.

- Unlike a typical one-hour dance class, a workshop may consist of more than two hours of learning. If instructors announce a one-hour workshop, it is really just a class.
- Although you can always learn something from different instructors at different dance workshops, you get more benefit taking private lessons and sharing the expense with your partner. You will spend the same amount as for a workshop, but you will learn more because you will get the undivided attention of the instructor, rather than getting a few minutes of attention during a workshop.
- If you take workshops from instructors from out of town without knowing their background, you may be wasting your time and money. Even though those instructors may be good dancers, it is important to take your own lessons locally, and use the workshops for additional training or for fun.
- Workshops are attended by some instructors because they want to learn new steps and improve their dance skills. These workshops may be intended for the training of instructors and may be of less value to students.
- Some instructors just like to teach new steps at workshops, rather than help the students to improve what they already know. For example, you may know many steps but have very little technique, style or understanding of the music. If you simply learn more steps without improving your technique, you may not be benefiting.
- You may enjoy taking dance lessons from many different instructors because you think you can learn and experience a variety of techniques and styles. You may, however, need to stick with a single instructor for most of your lessons to achieve a level of consistency.

Instructional Videos and Books

Dance videos: You can buy commercial videotapes that have been created by dance instructors.

Learning to dance from commercial videos can be less expensive and may be easy for a visually oriented individual with some dance experience. However, if you are a beginner, videos may not be the answer, because you do not yet have the feel for the steps. In that case, it is important that you have someone who is experienced in teaching to guide and support you as you learn how to dance through videos.

Before buying a dance videotape, look for the instructional technique that suits you best. In some instructional dance videos, one instructor explains the steps for both men and women, rather than a man explaining his steps and how to lead while a woman explains her steps and how to follow. Dance videos should include explanations and demonstrations by both men and women to encourage you to improve your dancing.

Books: You may learn to dance from books if you are an intellectual individual who likes to follow written instructions. However, it may take longer because there is no one to tell you whether you are doing it right or wrong. You may also have a difficult time learning to lead or follow your partner. Learning to dance from books requires some experience to understand the concept of communication and language on the dance floor.

Informal Instruction

(See the chapter on instructors).

Street Dance Instructors

Street instructors are those who have not had any formal dance training from studios or professional instructors. They have learned dancing by watching and teaching themselves and others, and have developed their own approach to teaching. Be aware of the following:

- Some street dance instructors do not use many verbal instructions; instead, they may prefer to dance and let students follow. These instructors may have problems breaking down the steps to help you learn them easily. This will be a disadvantage if you are the intellectual type, because you may need the verbal information or explanation to make a picture in your mind to do the step.
- You may take longer to learn how to dance from these instructors, because they may not know the dance syllabus, technique or style. They usually have more students who want to have fun dancing than becoming serious enough to be able to perform and compete. In contrast, trained instructors know both the men's and the women's steps and have more understanding of dance technique and style.
- Street instructors may not know the names of the steps they teach, and make up names for them. Later, if you start taking lessons at established dance studios where they use specific names for the dance steps and syllabus, you may become confused.

Glossary of Dance-related Terms

If you are aware of the concepts associated with ballroom dancing, eventually you can dance with anyone:

- Lead: To take control and initiate dance steps with your partner while navigating around the floor. Always allow your partner to finish her steps.

- Follow: Remain flexible and patient and wait for your partner's lead. Eye contact is important because it allows you to communicate more effectively.
- Frame: Physical resistance from your upper body in order to follow or lead.
- Posture: Proper posture and straight stance, with your shoulders slightly back.
- Balance: Keeping 80% of your weight on one leg and 20% on the other gives stability as you move across the floor.
- Momentum: Force of a moving body, continued movements in the same direction to create balance.
- Melody: Successions of musical notes, agreeable sound of the music fast, slow and long breaks.
- Tempo: Rate of speed of the music.
- Beat: Rhythmic stress in music
- Rhythm: Motion, regular succession of sound, or natural feel of the music.
- Technique: Precise and proper foot work of a dance.
- Style: Different personalities of dances.
- Social American ballroom versus International style.

The more you teach and share what you know,
the less you forget.
***

Your heart is the door to your soul and mind.
***

If you feel insecure about yourself,
you will feel insecure about your partner.
***

If you do not know what love is,
you cannot experience it.
***

Spirituality is your reality.
***

3

Chapter 3 Choosing an Instructor

Your instructor can be the most important asset in dancing because he/she can facilitate your self expression, develop your talents, and thus enable you to achieve your full potential as a dancer. Your instructor can help you become aware of your muscle coordination, balance, and posture, as well as become attuned to music as you learn to lead or follow. Dance can be a most powerful tool for you in realizing yourself, and your instructor is a key individual to help you get the most from that tool.

Teaching dancing can be one of life's most exciting adventures. It is an opportunity to help yourself and others to become happier individuals. A good and wise teacher in any field exhibits happiness, sensitivity, patience, perception, honesty, humor, health, and a flexible personality. With these qualities, your instructor will not merely teach you, but will promote enjoyment at the same time. To teach successfully, your instructor needs proper dance training, plenty of experience, a knowledge of dance history and music, and the ability to work with different people (honesty is another aspect of love). (Armed with these qualifications, an experienced instructor can attain strong relationships with his/her students and can work with them successfully in the long-term. Communication is one of the most important aspects).

Out-of-Town Instructors

Some instructors come from out of town or from other countries at the request of studios or private instructors. Sometimes these teachers may not even speak your language, in which case it can be difficult for you to learn everything, even if there are translators. If you are a beginner and an intellectual, you may find it more difficult to learn some steps, because you need verbal explanations to have a picture in your mind before doing the dance. However, if you are a visual dancer, you may be able to copy the steps without verbal communication. Remember that dancing is a universal language that can be communicated through your dance body movements, leading, following, and your passion. When a studio features a workshop from an out-of-town instructor, it should be considered an "extra" and not the principal way to learn, because there is no reinforcement possible after the event.

Teaching Approach

It is most important that you choose an instructor who is happy and loves his/her job. This instructor can give you more pleasure and more quality time during your lesson. If you choose an instructor who later shows his/her pessimistic or negative personality, this attitude may affect you. It can also be discouraging for you to hear your instructor using negative terms and phrases, such as "stupid," "dumb," "come on," or "no-no-no" when you make mistakes during private or group lessons. This will not help you develop confidence in your dancing. An instructor using these negative terms is releasing his/her anger at you. Instead, your instructor should encourage you to enjoy yourself while you are learning to dance in order for you to relax and become more receptive to new steps. This will enable you to become a more independent dancer, which later will make it much easier for you to dance with others. A good instructor will adapt to your personality in order to bring out your abilities during your lessons.

Beyond that, there are two kinds of instructors: the natural instructor and the normal instructor.

- Natural or feeling instructors are natural dancers who have natural rhythm. In other words, they move easily to music without thinking about it. They love their job as instructors and they can be very creative, which can make it more fun for you to learn. They enjoy teaching because they like to share their love of dancing. If you are a natural dancer, go to an instructor who is also a natural dancer to learn dancing in your own and natural way. Teaching dancing for this instructor is a pleasure as much as a job.

- Normal or intellectual instructors often are more restricted and may have less natural rhythm. In other words, they think before they move to the music. They can be excellent, but also more mechanical dancers in their approach, and may like to teach dancing exactly as they learned it because they like to follow structure. If you are a normal dancer, take lessons from those who are also normal dance instructors to learn dancing in your own and normal way. Teaching dancing for this instructor is a serious job.

Street Dancers Versus Trained Dancers

- Street dancers are those who have not had previous training and simply love to dance through their own inner and outer feelings. Their dance styles may be different, more enjoyable, flirtatious and entertaining than those who are trained, because they feel less restricted, or less inhibited.
- Trained dancers will have good technique, but are usually more rigid about their dancing, because they have learned restrictions, which in turn affects their freedom to express themselves naturally. Through experience they may become more joyful and natural dancers.

Being both a trained and a street dancer is, of course, ideal, so that you can express your innate passion for dance with eloquence.

The Thinker

An instructor who is a thinker can help you analyze the concept of a step or a dance, so you can create a picture in your mind before you do it or teach it. However, too much explanation from your instructor and not enough dancing or practice can lead you into an educational and stifled approach. Ballroom dancing requires both an educational and practical approach instead.

Trying to learn a lot of technique from a detail-oriented instructor at the beginner level may demand a lot of discipline on your part. At this level, the enjoyment of dancing may fade because you may feel under pressure during the beginning lessons, and pressure may become stressful. If you cannot relax while you learn, you may decide to quit dancing.

The Performer

An instructor who is also a performer and can communicate through actions has the ability to make you dance and move to the music without teaching you steps. However, if you feel that you are not getting enough verbal explanation or dance terminology from your instructor, you can always ask for some additional information on paper. For example, what a close position, (holding partner with one hand and embracing with the other) open position, (holding partner with one or two hands apart from each other) or free style position, (no holding partner's hands and apart from each other).

Too Much or Too Little

There is nothing wrong if your instructor is teaching you many steps in a few private lessons if you can learn them—videotaping your lessons may help you to remember. In fact, this can be an indication that your instructor is giving you all he/she has. If you are a fast learner, you can become a great dancer.

If your instructor spends too much time on basic steps when you have bought a package of private lessons, you can always ask to learn new steps if you think you are ready for more. You can also ask another instructor to check on your progress. However, learning too many steps, too much leading, following, technique, rhythm and more, can be demanding and overwhelming for you to handle all at once.

If you find that your instructor is confusing you by teaching too slowly or teaching more than you can handle in one lesson, ask yourself why. If you are concerned about the lessons, either his/her teaching style or his/her motives may be at fault.

- Does your instructor understand the pace at which you can learn?
- Does it look like you will have to stay with this instructor for a long time to cover everything he/she has planned?
- Do you think that your instructor is afraid of losing your business?
- Is your teacher covering details too soon?

Providing Fun

Time usually passes much more quickly when you and your instructor are having a good time during your private lesson. This usually happens when there is good chemistry between the two of you. On the other hand, when you and your instructor are having a hard time or feeling frustrated, the lesson goes much slower. This may happen because of the lack of chemistry between the two of you or because one of you is having a bad day. If your instructor does not have enough patience or understanding to cope with you, you may experience a lot of discomfort and eventually lose your temper and start a conflict, which can lead you to stop taking lessons.

It is also important that you encourage your instructor or studio to hire other instructors from out of town or exchange instructors to teach dance workshops. This will keep your interest as well as expose you to new steps and styles of dancing.

Instructors Should Continue their Training

Workshops provide an opportunity for instructors to become students again, learn more, and be critiqued by other professionals. Some instructors may not like to attend dance workshops, because they may feel uncomfortable taking it with other students or may worry that they may lose their reputations. However, training is always beneficial at every level because you never stop learning.

Important Characteristics for Both of You

No matter what kind of business or intellectual approach an instructor has in providing training, you need to look for the following characteristics, which are mandatory to both of you if you want to get the most from your lessons:

- Honesty and a sense of humor.
- Open-mindedness.
- Courtesy.
- Good manners.

Honesty and a sense of humor make it easier for you to learn to dance, because you are more receptive and relaxed. These qualities make for a beneficial dance environment. An instructor with these qualities generally loves his/her job. This does not mean that if your instructor has no sense of humor he/she cannot teach, but it can make dancing more fun and therapeutic for you if he/she has one.

When you and your instructor are open-minded during your lessons, your mistakes can inspire your instructor instead of frustrate him/her. For example, your error might inspire your instructor to create a new step or remind him/her of a step that he/she used to know. Therefore, your instructor should use the occasion for teaching you rather than becoming impatient. It is unprofessional for your instructor to take out anger or frustration on you. When your instructor goes through hard times in his/her personal life, it should not affect the work environment. That can only turn you off and make it more difficult to work together.

Courtesy is vital. The relationship between you and your

instructor should be friendly and unconditional, without taking each other for granted. For example, when you need to change your private lesson at the last minute because something important or an emergency has come-up, your instructor should be able to understand and not charge for the class. By the same token, when your instructor changes your private lesson at the last minute, it would also be nice for you to understand his/her situation. This is a good policy to establish between you and your instructor.

Good manners creates professionalism and respect between the two of you. Good manners leads to a good and friendly dance environment. It is important for everyone to know "The Law of Abundance" in the dance environment, because it can help all dancers and instructors to unite as one. Understanding this law, instructors realize they do not need to compete with each other, because there is enough of everything for everyone. There is no need to cheat on others in order to get more money nor to monopolize students, who after all, have the free will to do as they please. If your instructor or your partner believe in abundance he/she will share more with others.

Characteristics to Watch Out For

The following characteristics on the part of your instructor can interfere with your progress:

- Anger.
- No interest in upgrading own skills.
- Over-confidence.
- Stress.

It is not acceptable for your instructor to become angry when you make mistakes, because most people make mistakes when learning how to dance. Neither should he/she make any derogatory remarks about you or someone else. However, nega-

tive emotions can also be triggered by your own negative behavior, because anger triggers anger just as happiness triggers
happiness.

When your instructor is over-confident, he/she may treat
you without much respect, and start calling you with his/her
fingers, hands or by nicknames rather than by your name. In
addition, he/she may have the tendency to postpone your private lessons in order to schedule new students. This kind of
instructor is forgetting his/her responsibilities, and in the long
run, if you put up with this, you may become angry and bitter.

If your instructor has too many responsibilities and demands
on his/her time, it can affect your relationship. For example, if
your instructor has personal and financial problems, he/she may
be tempted to waste part of your lesson time discussing these
problems or may urge you to take extra lessons because he/she
needs money. Teaching dancing for more than 30 hours a week
can also be very tiring for your instructor. Therefore, you can try
to schedule your private lessons early in the week such as Mon-
day or Tuesday, and early in the evening or morning. This way
you have him/her fresh and rested.

If your instructor dislikes dancing with those who are physically unattractive or the elderly, he/she refuses to see the beauty
within these people. When they see beauty on the inside, they
also see it on the outside. This instructor may eventually have
very limited students because of this perception.

Impact of Your Own Personality

If your instructor is aware of your body type or your personality, it can help you to improve your dance style and your
attitude towards your dancing. For example, if you are a clumsy
or passive individual who has no grace when you dance, or
you have a hard time learning fancy steps or dance styles, it
may be because you are holding back your passion for dancing or life. Your muscle coordination may not be coordinated

with your mind, because your body, mind and soul are not integrated. If you are an emotional individual, you may be impulsive, allowing your body to move on its own, creating a different and awkward body language. When you are dancing with your partner, you may be moving ahead, making him/her think that you are anticipating or leading. Your instructor can help you smooth your body language to help you gain more control by having you close your eyes and drag your feet when dancing slowly, so you can be totally and more consciously aware of your body movements. Later, this training can help you to coordinate your body and your mind.

Keep in mind that your own personality can also make a difference in finding the right instructor: When you are ready to improve your dancing or your life, the teacher will come to you, because what you project, you also attract.

- If you are very active and assertive, find an instructor with a similar personality. If you work with a passive or quiet individual instructor, you may become restless, because you may not have enough patience.
- If you have a passive personality, try to work with an active and assertive instructor so you can achieve balance and express yourself differently and be more communicative with your partners.
- If you are a shy dancer, you may be lacking self-confidence and interaction with others. The best way to overcome this shyness is to take 30 to 50 private lessons, as well as group classes so that you will feel encouraged to practice with others.
- If you are an aggressive dancer, you might intimidate your partner with a strong or heavy lead or by not following well. Your instructor might help you become less aggressive by asking you to dance with your eyes closed, so you can relax and stop being too judgmental of the outside world or to others. You need an instructor

to help you free yourself from the many restrictions you have placed on yourself in order for you to see the beauty within yourself, and the beauty in others.

Emulating Your Partners' Personalities

Have you ever wondered why your personality changes with certain partners or people while interacting or dancing? The reason is because you are reacting to their personalities and changing your attitude for no apparent reason.

The following are examples of how you may react and how to deal with negative or positive situations:

- If you become friendly with your partner or instructor for no apparent reason, enjoy the company or the lessons. With the same token they are reminding you of *who you are*.
- If you find yourself in a bad mood or react defensively with your instructor or partner for no apparent reason, this is an indication that you are reacting and experiencing your own pain triggered by him/her.
- If you are feeling intimidated or afraid of your instructor or partner for no apparent reason, watch out. He/she may be trying to dominate you and take advantage of you.
- If you become sexually turned on by your partner or instructor, this is a sign that the two of you have strong chemistry for each other—enjoy the dancing. If you become romantically involved with your instructor, be aware that it may simply be your love for dance that is making you project your feelings onto him/her.

Instructors You May Be Drawn To

Often you unconsciously attract instructors or partners with a similar personality as your own. Sometimes you may think that you attract the opposite in partners. In reality you have suppressed or repressed what your instructor has developed. Therefore, you are attracting what you need to work on.

- If you keep finding yourself attracting instructors with assertive personalities, it is because you may be holding back this aspect of yourself and being shy. You are unconsciously or consciously creating this attraction in order to improve yourself and become more balanced.
- If you have the tendency to attract happy instructors or partners, it is because you are also happy or want to bring out your own happiness.
- If you attract angry instructors or partners, it is because you are also an angry person. In other words, others are opening your eyes to remind you that you need to improve yourself and let go of your judgment of others. When you remove your judgment, you will remove your pain or anger and attract different kinds of people.
- If you attract intellectual instructors, you like instructors to explain the steps in great detail before demonstrating them, so you can visualize them. You are going to attract instructors with comparable personalities to your own. Instructors usually call you politely by your last name because of the distance and manner you are projecting. Instructors of this type like to remain emotionally distant from you too, because for them this interaction is mainly business. These instructors may have a hard time getting any more intimate with you.
- If you attract physically demonstrative instructors, you may like your instructor to demonstrate the steps while describing them, because the verbal or intellectual instructions may not be enough for you. You like to watch your instructor doing the step so you can copy him/her. Your instructor may also enjoy using his/her hands to explain the steps. In addition, if you are a mentally, physically, and emotionally balanced dancer, you will attract these types of instructors or partners.

Needs of Natural Dancers

Natural dancers or instructors are those who consciously express and project their passion, feelings, and body movements through music directly to themselves, their partners, or to the audience. These dancers or instructors have the tendency to express the melody more than tempo of the music, so they have more variation of movements than just a consecutive set of rigid steps. If you are a street dancer who has learned by watching others and likes to improvise, you may be a natural dancer. You like to show your talent and dance differently with different partners because each one inspires you uniquely. Therefore, you may need to find an instructor who feels the music and can help you bring out more of yourself.

An instructor who teaches you to dance on the second beat (in the International style of ballroom dance) may make you feel awkward or unnatural. You may have difficulty following the music, because you are a feeling dancer. Therefore, you feel the music on the first beat or the strong beat. If you feel the music, it is hard to ignore and may get in your way when you are busy concentrating on your steps or if your instructor is teaching you only the steps and patterns. Some instructors suggest that steps be learned first without music, and later, as you feel more comfortable with the steps, you can begin to listen to the music.

In addition, it is important to avoid instructors who try to keep you from enjoying yourself when you train for competitions, because they may think that you should be serious and not improvise your dance routines. You can always be trained for competitions, but you should also be able to be yourself and have fun on the dance floor. Your instructors should always use and work with your natural talents as a natural dancer rather than push you to be too competitive and serious. They may not realize that they are making you repress your enjoyment.

Tips for Normal Dancers to Become Natural Dancers

Normal dancers or instructors are those who are intellectually expressing what they have learned mechanically from conventional dance studios or private instructors. These instructors at the studios may teach steps, technique, and style without much attitude, feeling or passion for dancing. The following are suggestions to help you get in touch with your feelings so that you can feel the music especially if you are living in a high stress environment:

- Becoming in Touch with Music: With your eyes closed, listen to your favorite music to help you get in touch with your soul, mind and body. Later, your body will naturally respond to the beat or melody of the music. In addition, close your eyes while dancing with a partner to help you relax, feel the music and think less. The less distractions you have the more in touch you become with your inner world or feelings.
- Improving Muscle Coordination: Learn tap dancing or drumming to help you acquire muscle coordination.
- Stress Reduction: Have weekly spiritual healing or energy work such as Reiki to help you release your repressed emotions so you can improve your passion for dance or life. All repressed emotions can block you from feeling the music and enjoying yourself.

Sex of the Instructor

There are different advantages to working with a man or a woman. It is for the student to decide.

Learning from a Man

If you are a man, learning to dance from another man can be as easy as learning from a woman. However, not all men feel comfortable dancing with another man, because they may be reluctant to have body contact due to their upbringing. An experienced instructor is always recommended if you decide to work with another man.

To begin with, the two of you can hold each other's shoulders while your instructor does the woman's steps and tells you verbally what to do. Later, you can hold your instructor as you would hold a female partner and do the steps. During your lessons, your instructor can explain his views about leading and executing the steps. He can tell you how to lead different women.

Later, your instructor or you can invite a female student to practice with you and see how you do. Leading a woman should require less effort on your part after you have been dancing with your male instructor.

If you are a woman, learning to dance from a man can be as easy as learning from another woman, because it can help you understand how men think on the dance floor. In other words, you will experience men's physical strength or leading while dancing with you, while women instructors are usually more gentle when dancing with another woman.

Learning from a Woman

Taking lessons from a woman, on the other hand, enables a man to learn the woman's point of view, and to understand the need for different leads. For example, women who are passive need a semi-strong lead in order to move at an even speed with you. Women who are active, assertive or aggressive may need a soft lead because they are more aware and experienced. Those women who like to take the lead need more space to improvise and to do their own steps. Although women who are domineering may have a hard time interacting with you, only one may lead on the dance floor and it is usually the man.

If you are a woman, you may have an easier time learning from someone of the same sex. In general, women tend to understand and relate more effectively to each other than men do. However, it is always best to have some exposure to both male and female instructors.

Other Gender-Related Differences

Women generally enjoy taking dance lessons from men, women, and gay professionals because they are not as threatened as men of reversing gender roles.

Men should not underestimate gay instructors however. If you are a man and reluctant to work with a gay male because you feel you are too macho or are not open to their life-style, you may be losing an opportunity to learn from fine dancers.

If you enjoy working with gay instructors, a gay instructor can work well with you because you can learn a more feminine style through him/her. If you are the aggressive type, you may need a passive gay instructor to bring more gentle balance on the dance floor. If you are a passive or shy person, a gay instructor with confidence can teach you to be more assertive.

A bisexual instructor can also teach both men and women students. By accepting their dance talents, you can learn a great deal of dance style because they have experienced both gender aspects.

Evaluating an Instructor

After determining your own requirements for an instructor, you can begin to evaluate candidates:

- Before you begin to take lessons, it is important for you to know a dance instructor's background and whether you feel comfortable with that instructor. Your level of comfort is key to finding the learning situation you need.
- Always choose an instructor on the basis of the instructor's philosophies and the dance styles and techniques that are offered. That will enable you to understand what you are learning and to become a more comfortable dancer. Ask friends who dance well who the good instructors are, and begin finding out more about them.
- If you are a serious dancer and want to compete, you should work with someone who is also serious and competitive. See where he/she trained, what awards they have achieved, etc. If you just want to have fun, this is not a factor. This pairing by compatibility will greatly accelerate the rate at which you progress in your dancing.
- It is not how many dance lessons you take that is important, but how aware you are of your own body language in dancing. Becoming aware of your dance movements or posture allows you to pay more attention to your muscle memory so you can learn to dance faster. For example, do you have the tendency to tilt forward or backward when you dance? Do you dance on your toes? Do you think a lot when you follow or lead?

Try to find the best instructors in your own area and follow up your classes before seeking instructors from out of town. Try to get instruction from both men and women, because you can undoubtedly benefit from the differences in their perspectives. Male and female instructors may have different insights into leading and following.

If you are single, you may attract single instructors because the two of you can relate similarly to each other. However, even if you are married, you may enjoy having a single instructor because of the good chemistry between you.

Here are more pointers for women:

- To determine whether a male instructor has great style, ask him to do the women's steps and styling with another male. This can be an opportunity to find out if you like his style of dancing or teaching or think it is suitable for you.
- If your instructor enjoys women's company, you may get along quite well with him, because he may understand your needs in dancing. This can help you learn to bring out more of your feminine side on the dance floor.
- If your instructor has a tendency to teach you more than he/she is supposed to or likes to keep you dancing for several minutes after your private lesson is over or likes to teach you at clubs or studios, it is because your instructor likes your company. However, if there is not enough chemistry between you, he/she may only dance with you once at a dance practice. If you are sensitive about rejection, this may diminish your confidence.

Chemistry Between You and Your Instructor

Good chemistry between you and your instructor can help you learn dancing faster because of the similarity in personality. As a result of this chemistry, you can become a feeling dancer. But the same chemistry can also complicate your relationship.

Unfortunately, some instructors may not know how to help you get in touch with your feelings while dancing, because they are trained to teach you steps. As a result, you may have the tendency to dance without paying too much attention to the music, because you are always involved with your steps and your partner. However, as a beginner, you may have to pass through several stages before you can express your feelings and become a natural, feeling dancer.

Long-Term Relationship with Your Instructor

Once you have found a suitable instructor, working with the same one for a long time can have definite advantages. One of the main advantages is that you will get more than you expect from this teacher. The following are guidelines that will help you establish and preserve a long-term relationship:

- Use good manners.
- Acknowledge your mistakes.
- Ask your instructor to take you and other students dancing to different places.
- Break and make some rules in order to get along.
- Develop a friendship.
- Develop a peaceful interaction with your teacher.
- Do not let it bother you if your instructor is having a bad day.
- Do not believe everything you hear about your instructor.
- Encourage your instructor to do his/her job cheerfully so you can have fun together.
- Do not judge your instructor, only observe his/her actions.
- Share your dance dreams with him/her.
- Treat him/her with honesty, kindness, patience, gentleness, understanding, and humor.

Cancellations

A cancellation at the last minute can be inconvenient for both the student and the instructor because it wastes time and money.

If your instructor or student cancels the private lesson at the last minute or a few hours before without giving you an excuse, this may indicate that he/she has more important things to do than the private lesson. If it happens several times, consider finding someone else. It is important that the instructor or the student stick with his/her responsibilities. Your instructor may have a policy of charging you if you cancel your private lesson at the last minute or a few hours before. If your instructor does not show up or cancels your private lesson without a legitimate excuse, you should have a free private lesson. If your instructor or student cancels the private lesson due to an emergency, it is acceptable not to charge. If you are 15 minutes late for your private lesson you are entitled to get a 45 minute lesson. But if your instructor does not have another student afterwards, it is his/her prerogative to give you the full hour.

In addition, if your instructor is feeling under the weather, it is his/her responsibility to let you know before you come to class. For instance, if your instructor has a virus that can be contagious, your instructor should call you and let you know that he/she is ill. This way you can make a decision whether to take the class or postpone it. You, as a student should do the same for your instructor.

Freelance Instructors

Freelance dance instructors, or independent instructors, are often trained instructors who used to work for major or small dance studios and later became independent. This kind of instructor may enjoy helping you more than an instructor employed by a conventional dance studio, since a freelancer does not have to follow as many rules, contracts or policies as do dance studio staff members. Working one-on-one with a freelancer is helpful when you have extra problems to overcome, such as shyness or an aggressive approach to dancing, because they are usually flexible about what to spend time on during the lesson.

If you are Planning to be Freelance Instructor

- Create a name for your dance company.
- Get permission or a license to teach at home through the county you live in.
- Open a business and credit merchant account at your nearby bank to allow students to pay with credit cards.
- Let the contracts be optional and flexible for your students.
- Register with the National Dance Council of America or others in order to participate at dance competitions.
- Learn the dance syllabus that is required by the National Dance Council of America.
- Advertise your dance classes through the internet, business cards, word of mouth, and flyers.
- Always be on time for your lessons.
- Have flexible hours for lessons on the weekdays or weekends.
- Rent other places or studios by the hour to teach your dance classes or private lessons.
- Schedule all your group and private lessons in a book.
- Sound equipment or boom-boxes are essential.
- You can teach on the ground level in your apartment or in your house.
- You may charge $40 to $95 an hour, depending on your experience.

Believe in abundance so you will not compete or fight with other teachers or studios to recruit new students. Allow your students to come and go of their own free will.

It takes effort to make things look effortless.
***

Everyone brings you awareness, be alert.
***

You are not your past, only your now.
***

Impatience leads to frustrations.
***

Believing is seeing.
***

4

Chapter 4 Expenses

Cost of Lessons

When discussing the cost of dance lessons with your prospective instructor, do not be too stingy or tight. If you seem not to value the lessons enough to pay what they cost, the instructor may lose interest in giving you quality lessons. You may not appreciate nor understand what professionals have to go through to work with you. A good and experienced instructor not only helps you to learn how to dance but can also help you build up your confidence. The bottom line is, if an instructor accepts a lower rate from you, you may be getting inferior lessons. If you try to learn dancing on your own to avoid the cost without a professional, you may have a hard time dancing with others, because you are not getting the foundations of leading and following.

In some instances, you do not need to have money to get private or group dance lessons. You may have a talent that you can use to exchange services with an instructor. For example, a massage therapist can exchange private dance lessons for a full body massage; an accountant can fill out tax forms for two or three private dance lessons; a dressmaker can make a dance outfit for two or more private lessons; and so on. There are infinite ways for dance students to get dance lessons in exchange for professional services. All it takes is asking.

Ripping You Off

If you find that your instructor went bankrupt after you have made a large payment for your dance lessons, it is not worth becoming stressed or vengeful at him/her for the loss of money. The next time you want to invest money in dance classes, make sure to pay for 10 or 20 private lessons at a time; this way you do not have to pay too much up front. Finish taking 10 or 20 private lessons and then write a check for the next 10 or 20 lessons. This way if you are planning to stay with your instructor for several years, you are getting the best rate while promoting a good relationship with him/her.

Videos of Your Own Lessons

You may not like watching yourself dancing on a videotape, because you may feel embarrassed, lack self-confidence, dislike your physical appearance or have repressed fears about your identity. However, watching yourself on videotape with a professional for feedback can be an excellent way to monitor your progress on steps, technique, and style, and to learn to appreciate yourself and your dance body language. In addition, a video of you dancing with someone who is experienced, or with an instructor, may look very different from you dancing with another novice. Your instructor can always make you look more advanced. Videotaping your dance lessons is always good because it can later help remind you of steps you may forget.

Some instructors or studios may not charge to videotape your private lesson if you buy a package of 10 or more lessons and may even supply the videotapes. Other instructors or studios may charge additional money for the use of their equipment to videotape your private lessons.

Dance Shoes

Good dance shoes are expensive (usually $90 or more) but are important for dance instructors and students, because they are both flexible and comfortable (psychologically they can promote the feeling that you are a real dancer). However, some dancing shoes with very thin soles can damage the feet by causing blisters, especially when dancing for more than several hours at a time. By adding extra padding in the shoes, dancers can be a lot more comfortable for long hours of dancing. Dance supply stores as well as vendors at dance competitions offer a variety of professional quality dance shoes.

Shoes are covers for the feet, but how you wear your shoes may say something about yourself:

- If you wear your shoes tightly laced, you like security and tend to be hard on yourself (because you are squeezing your feet). The tighter the shoes are fastened, the less chance they have of coming off, but eventually there is discomfort when your feet swell.
- If you tend to wear loafer shoes while dancing, you are more practical, flexible, and perhaps somewhat lazy.
- If you wear high-heeled shoes, they can cause you to lean forward, putting more weight and pressure on your knees and toes. These shoes can tire your feet sooner if you wear them all the time. Limit yourself to two-inch heels if you practice or dance long hours.
- If you like to wear metal heel-plates on your shoes, you are probably looking for recognition or showing authority. This can be dangerous for inexperienced dancers because they can slip.
- If you are dancing on the carpet, wear regular leather sole shoes. If you are dancing on a wood floor, wear suede shoes for good traction.
- If you are dancing on concrete, wear rubber sole shoes.

- If you have short legs, tan color dance shoes can make your legs look longer. Dark shoes can make your legs look shorter. Closed-toed dancing shoes will protect you from others stepping on your feet. Open-toed shoes are best for Latin dances since the toes can spread out for balance.
- If you want your comfortable walking or tennis shoes to become your dance shoes, let your shoemaker glue suede soles onto your old shoes. This may bring some psychological comfort while you are learning.

Where to Go Dancing

Admission to Dance Floors

The owners of dance studios, nightclubs or restaurants have to pay high rent. That is why the cost is passed to the consumer. However, some people offer dance practice at their homes, where they usually ask dancers to bring drinks or food to share. This can cost a lot less than paying $10 or $15 for admission.

Nightclubs and Restaurants

Some dancers go to nightclubs, where they pay very little money to get in, but find the place either too crowded, a meat market, or filled with cigarette smoke. Furthermore, the dance floor is seldom large. Nightclubs are moneymakers and are designed to have very small dance floors and a lot of tables to sit, eat, smoke and drink. People who dance should realize that most nightclubs make money from alcohol.

If your instructor takes you and a group of people out dancing to a club, it is best to go to early in the evening from 7:30 to 10:30 P.M. when it is less crowded. During this time there is more room on the dance floor to practice.

On occasion, you may find yourself dancing very little during these practice sessions, because some pirate dancers have left your group without partners. "Pirate dancers" are individuals who take your partners away from your group, making you wait for a while before you can dance with a partner. However, you can agree with other students to stay together beforehand in order to avoid interaction with pirate dancers unless they are your friends. After 10 P.M., you and your instructor can have the freedom to dance and socialize with anyone. In fact, your instructor may enjoy dancing with other instructors from the same or different studios to show their talents or attract more business.

Dance Studios

Dance studios offer a much more inviting and beneficial experience for dance practice because of the quality of the floor, the large space, and the seriousness of the dancers. Some studios charge an admission of $10 to $15. The price often includes a dance class, three hours of general dance practice, and some soft drinks and snacks.

If you do not know yourself, how can you be yourself?

***

Awareness, decisions, and actions can move you anywhere you want to go.

***

You can only have fun now, not later.

***

Change, brake, and make new rules so you can experience harmony.

***

Repetition produces recognition.

***

5

Chapter 5 What to Expect from Your Lessons

Your characteristics as a student have an impact on the kind of instruction you need and what you should expect from a lesson. The same is true if you are arranging for lessons for someone else. This chapter describes what to expect and what to watch for, depending on who you are or who you are arranging lessons for, and whether you have chosen to learn through private lessons or in a class as part of a group.

Preparing for Your Lesson

It is important to warm-up or stretch before dance lessons or practice and Yoga can be a most effective stretching exercise.

It is important for you to spend a few minutes communicating with your instructor before lessons. This can help you understand each other and be more relaxed and comfortable. Besides, talking while dancing may be difficult or impossible for you until you have had some experience.

Before buying dance classes, ask your instructor to tell you the benefits of dancing, so you have a different idea of what you want to work on. For example, fast dances can help you to reduce the amount of fat on your body or lose weight or increase your good cholesterol. It can also improve your cardiovascular system and muscle coordination, increase your emotional, physical, and mental strength, and build self-confidence. Slow or smooth dances can help you learn to control your balance and emotions. Make sure your instructor allows you to choose the dance and style you want to learn; and if you do not know much about it, then let your instructor recommend some popular dances. However, you may just want to take dance lessons for pleasure and the social benefits, in which case, you just want to hear the music that you love and enjoy learning the dance steps.

During your lesson, the following can help you get the most for your time and money:

- Do not wear clothes that are tight or confining or you may have difficulty moving.
- Do not wear beaded dresses, shirts, or blouses that can be uncomfortable for your partner's hands while dancing.
- Do not wear running or tennis shoes during your lessons, because it can make it harder to slide on the floor.
- Do not have other students present during your lessons if you are a shy person; one-on-one may be best for you in a private room.
- Do not wear jewelry such as sharp rings or necklaces or buckles that may hurt or bother your instructor or partner during the lesson or practice.
- Do not chew gum or eat during your dance class, because it creates distractions and may prevent you from hearing instructions clearly.

Taking Private Lessons

Your first private lesson is the most important because you are going to find out how your instructor connects with you, and how he/she is going to teach.

One-on-one private lessons with an instructor of the opposite sex can be more enjoyable when there is good chemistry between the two of you. Chemistry can be based on personal qualities, such as warmth, the love of fun, artistic interests, and other affinities, like emotional or intellectual makeup or personality type.

The advantage of taking private lessons is that you can learn faster, develop more technique and style by having all of the instructor's attention and thus gain more confidence than you can taking group classes. The following is the easiest and most comfortable way to acquire a solid foundation:

- During the first set of 5 private lessons, you can learn 5 to 10 basic steps of two dances.
- During the second set of 5 private lessons, you can learn style, leading or following.
- During the third set of 5 private lessons, you can learn and understand the rhythm, melody, and tempo of the music.
- During the fourth set of 5 private lessons, you can learn to improvise in your dancing or demonstrate a routine with your instructor or a partner at classes, private social parties or beginner dance competitions.

At this point, you may understand what it means to be a dancer and you will have an appreciation for dancers who are more advanced than you are. You will also recognize those who are less technical and stylish than you are.

A lot can be covered in a one-hour private lesson when you are experienced. You can suggest that your instructor videotape your private lesson; reviewing the tape can help you remember the steps and the instructor's suggestions and demonstrations that you might otherwise forget. Watching yourself dancing on video may help you to correct your posture and style, and you will probably see improvements on your tapes after the fifth lesson.

If you are an instructor taking private lessons from another instructor, it can be very challenging if you each have different opinions about teaching dancing. For example, if you are an experienced, open minded instructor while the other instructor is more idealistic and rigid in his/her teaching methods, this may create tension between the two of you. However, if you are paying for the lessons, you can always demand what you want to learn. Otherwise, find someone else who will accommodate you.

Couples

Taking private lessons with a partner or spouse can be beneficial, especially if you practice between lessons.

If you and your partner get along well, teaching you to dance can be very enjoyable for your instructor, because it will be easy to work with you. Compatibility with your partner helps the two of you learn faster, and your instructor can observe you closely.

However, if you and your partner do not get along well during the lesson, it can be very challenging for your instructor, because he/she has to play referee during your disagreements. For example, if your female partner is not following your lead, but is anticipating the steps, following the music but not you, or is trying to lead, your instructor must take control of the situation and make your partner aware of her role on the dance floor. Free style dancing would be ideal for this follower because she will not need to follow her partner too closely.

Having a regular partner can help you to learn faster if the two of you practice enough outside the class. For this reason you might prefer not to change partners during the class, even though your instructor may encourage you to. On the other hand, if you feel uncomfortable changing partners because you do not like to share your partner with others, just take private lessons. Be aware of the benefits of learning to dance with other people however, before limiting yourself to one partner while you learn.

Lessons together can be an advantage for couples, but can also change relationships. For example, if your partner is more passive than you are and learns to become more assertive through dancing and the instructor's assistance, it can change your relationship. Later your partner may become mentally and emotionally stronger than before and start confronting you more often. In other words, you may have been mentally and emotionally stronger than your partner because of your domineering personality, but your partner is regaining confidence in his/her own identity and becoming as strong as you are. You may be disappointed at first, because you may be losing control over your partner or the relationship, but in the long run you will appreciate him/her as a mature and more advanced dancer. This change can bring some conflicts between the two of you for a while. Later, you may be more equal, and will have a different and healthier relationship. For example, your instructor can help make your partner a stronger leader and more assertive on the dance floor. After 10 or more private lessons, your partner may begin to confront you without realizing it. This image of a leader has given him more self-esteem to stand up for his role in dancing. If you find yourself suddenly wanting to quit the lessons, it may be because you want to maintain control over your partner or spouse.

There are other instances when one of you gets more attention from your instructor while taking a private lesson. This attitude by your instructor can diminish the relationship between the three of you and eventually cause you to stop the dance lessons. For example, if a female instructor has the tendency to give more attention to the woman than the man, this may indicate that this instructor may have unresolved issues with men or ex-dance partners. Perhaps there are power control issues between the man and the instructor or there is no chemistry between them. On the other hand, if a male instructor gives more attention to the man than the woman, this instructor may have unresolved problems with other women or ex-dance partners. Instructors whether they are men or women should always give equal attention to each student regardless of their levels of dancing experience.

Helping a Loved One Learn to Dance

Teaching your spouse or significant other to dance can be a most challenging task. Since there are no emotional boundaries between the two of you, it is easy for one of you to become angry or impatient with the other if you make mistakes during lessons or practice. Also if the two of you hear music differently, or have different interests or agendas in your dancing, it can be difficult for one of you to teach the other. A student and instructor working together would have an easier time: the student is paying for the lesson, so the instructor has to hold his/her temper to ease the situation.

Taking Group Lessons

The atmosphere at your first group lesson can be very crucial; often this is where you decide whether to continue the lessons, go elsewhere, or drop dancing entirely. The way your instructor introduces the lessons, adjusts them for the group, and handles the finances can make a big difference.

Finances

- If, at the first lesson, your instructor asks you to wait and pay at the end, he/she is being considerate of you. He/she is giving you a chance to try the first lesson before you buy the package or pay for one class at a time. However, if your instructor asks you to pay beforehand, he/she is not giving you a chance to try the class and decide whether you want to stay or not. You may ask your instructor to let you pay after the group lesson if you do not know him/her.
- If you come from out of town, and your instructor does not charge you for the first group lesson, it is his/her way of saying "welcome". But if you keep coming back to his/her classes, the instructor will charge you.
- If your instructor does not charge your relatives for the first group lesson because they are visiting you from another city or country, you are seeing a good quality in your instructor. This practice can also help your instructor fill in for a shortage of men or women.

Teaching Style

- If your instructor uses positive encouragement to help you feel at ease and comfortable while you learn, it is a good indication that he/she may be an experienced and patient instructor. In addition, if your instructor teaches or demonstrates a variety of dance styles to the class, he/she is being flexible and will allow you to choose the style you want to learn.

- If your instructor tends to spend more than 10 minutes explaining what not to do, he/she is paying too much attention to negatives in his/her personal life. By the time your instructor finishes explaining what not to do, you will have forgotten what you were supposed to have learned in the first place. This unfortunate behavior can try your patience, because you came to class to learn how to dance and not to hear complaints or his/her negative perceptions about dancing.

Adjustments for the Group

- If you find that your class has a larger number of women than men, it is important that your instructor ask the group to rotate partners so everyone gets an equal opportunity to choose a different partner and dance. However, if there are more women than men in the group, your instructor might also encourage you to take two partners and dance with them at the same time, in an open (holding partner by the hand) or free style position (no hand holding with your partner). This can help men feel good about themselves, because they can develop more self-confidence and become more developed leaders by using both hands. Likewise, if there are more men than women in the group, women can dance with two men at the same time. If women like to lead, this can be very enjoyable and an opportunity to experience what is usually the man's role.
- Your instructor should always make men and women switch partners during a group lesson. This way they can have the choice to dance with anyone they like.
- If you are a beginning level student, dancing with an intermediate level partner forces you to pay a lot more attention, and can help you to improve faster.

- If you are an intermediate level student and do not like to dance with beginners, your instructor may encourage you to dance with them anyway. Doing so can help you to develop leading or following skills, because you have to lead or follow your partner a little harder when the partner is less experienced.

- If you are an advanced level student ask your instructor to let you help teach the class. This can help you develop some experience in teaching beginner level students, and your instructor may not charge you for the class because you are helping him/her. You can always volunteer to assist when the class is too large. This will prevent the other students from getting discouraged by the size of the group and fearing that they will not get enough attention.

- If your instructor has a mix of young and old students in the group, with ranging tastes in music, he/she should play a variety of music to appeal to everyone. In swing lesson, for instance, the majority of the young crowd usually wants to hear modern music, while the majority of the older crowd may prefer to hear big band music, because it brings them back memories.

- It is important that your instructor encourage you to learn both to lead and to follow, so you can understand both viewpoints. Allowing women to learn how to lead and men to learn how to follow during group classes can be a lot of fun, because it can give you more awareness in the dance environment. If you are a domineering woman, this can be your chance to give men a good lead. If you are a passive woman, this is your chance to be more in control as you learn how to lead; if you refuse to lead, you just may not be ready to change yet. If you are an aggressive man, this can be your chance to relax and let your partner do the leading. If you refuse to be led by women, your ego is getting in the way. If you are a passive man, on the other hand, you may like your partner to do the work on the dance floor.

Expect the following from group classes:

- During the first 6 group classes, you may be able to learn the basic steps of one or two dances and several steps.
- During the 12 group classes, you may be able to learn to lead and follow.
- During the 18 group classes, you can learn more about music, such as how to follow the rhythm, melody, and tempo.
- During the 24 group classes, you may become comfortable with your dancing in two dances.

Personal Adjustment

The following sections discuss the needs of different age groups and personality types and what they should look for during a private lesson or group class.

Older Students

If you have a hard time being told what to do by a younger instructor during your private lesson, you may have too strong of an ego. It may be difficult for you to learn much from younger instructors, but there are things you can both do to make the lessons feel more comfortable and successful. If you call your instructor by his/her last name, he/she may also call you by your last name creating a more respectful atmosphere. Be patient and give the instructor a chance to show his/her experience. Later as you gain some confidence with your instructor, you can allow him/her to call you by your first name. If age continues to bother you, it is important that your instructor be close to your age, a few years younger or older, for you to feel comfortable while learning to dance.

Older instructors who have been teaching for a long time on the other hand, often do not have enough patience with beginners, younger professionals or amateurs during private lessons. These instructors may have high expectations of themselves and you. You do not need to be treated like a child when you make mistakes or cannot get the step right. You may speak out or find someone else.

Casual Students

If you just want to enjoy the lesson with your partner rather than focusing too much on steps, technique, styling or preparing to compete, let your instructor know that you just want to become a fair dancer and have fun. Your instructor can adjust the teaching approach and the content of the lessons to meet your goals.

"Take-Charge" Students

If you have a strong ego, especially if you own a business and are accustomed to being in control, it may be hard for you to be told what to do. You may also find yourself asking an excessive number of questions about your instructor before the lesson, instead of using the lessons themselves to find out for yourself how good he/she is. Some instructors may have less experience than others, yet still teach well because of their ability to communicate with simplicity and accuracy. Talk about this with your instructor, so he/she can take your feelings into account and teach you in a way that is acceptable to you.

Students from Other Cultures

If you are a new dance student from Japan, China, Thailand or other Asian country, you may be quite conservative when it comes to dancing. Therefore, if you find yourself physically uncomfortable when you get close to a partner, it may be because of your family or cultural background. In this situation, it is important to tell your instructor that you consider physical body contact too intimate for public places. Your instructor can explain this in class and let you decide how close you want to get to your partner especially if you have not lived long enough in places where there is more freedom to express oneself.

Minors

If you are under eighteen years of age or are arranging for lessons for a teenager or child, it is important to have an adult watch the lesson. A student who does not know the instructor too well may feel safer under these circumstances. It is also appropriate to bring a family member or a friend to watch the dance lesson and be entertained. If your instructor feels uncomfortable having others observe your private lesson, this is an indication that this instructor is not too experienced or may be hiding something.

Groups of Teenagers

Encouraging children to learn dance as a sport from kindergarten all the way to college can be a most valuable tool to help develop social skills. For example, if children were given 15 minutes to dance with each other every day or every other day at school, it could help them to express their joy and celebrate life.

Often teenagers take lessons with a group of friends. Sometimes the class includes 20 to 40 children from age 10 to 14. This is one of the most challenging classes one instructor can teach alone. It demands a great deal of patience, understanding, and other dance assistants. Teaching them to dance with fun and a sense of humor can be the most powerful approach. Children this age are noisy and easily distracted, and want to be among their peers, away from parents. At this age, they may be more interested in having fun, making faces, pushing their partners around or jumping like kangaroos, which is quite natural. However, because they just want to play, they may not be learning much dancing nor listening to the instructor in class. Furthermore, this behavior may prevent youngsters learning and accomplishing what parents are paying for.

It is important that parents know how the lessons are conducted and whether they are meeting expectations. During the first few classes, it is well to attend discreetly, in order to monitor your teenager's progress and interaction with others as well as with the instructor.

Instructors who already have children of their own may find it easier to teach your teenager, because they may have already taught their own children. During the lesson, the instructor's patience, understanding, and humor can help a teen-ager learn without stress or pressure.

It is also important that the instructor not become too serious, stress technique or styling too much or push teenagers too hard in the early lessons, because they may become discouraged. If your teenagers want to become more serious, private lessons can help them to become more advanced dancers and to develop style, personality, and originality. Through dancing, your teenagers can learn coordination and maintain good physical and mental health.

Challenged Individuals and Groups

Today, there are many organizations helping people in wheelchairs to improve themselves physically and mentally through a variety of exercise. In some cases, these physically challenged individuals are becoming professional runners on wheels, which gives them much more identity in society. If you have friends who are mentally or physically challenged, you can give them gift certificates for dance lessons to improve their image and self-confidence.

If you are mentally or physical challenged, dancing can help you to increase your physical and mental fitness, provide you with a means to become a competitor, and help you regain a most valued element of life, your joy for dancing.

Good intentions and patience are important qualities for your instructor. Your instructor may need a lot of patience to continually encourage you to dance and to help you have fun while you are learning. Teaching you to improvise in your dancing can help you become more creative and resourceful in other areas of life. Encouraging you to sing while dancing can also help you to become verbally more assertive, and ten minutes of exercising with your feet and hands before dancing can help your muscle coordination. For example, sit with your feet flat on the floor and tap your feet: right toe, left toe, right toe and left heel (1,2,3,4), repeating these exercises three or more times. Then, tap the opposite way with the left toe, right toe, left toe and right heel. This exercise can help you coordinate your mind and body movements. Tap dancing can also be an excellent exercise.

Mentally Challenged Students

It may be irrelevant to teach a lot of technique or style to the physically and mentally challenged, because they may lack the muscle coordination or muscle memory necessary for learning these fine points. It is more important that the instructor make the dance classes fun. They need a lot of love and attention–hugs while greeting them, a pat on the back when they accomplish something, such as a dance routine, or compliments about their appearance. Giving physical and mental attention to the mentally and physically challenged can encourage them to continue trying to dance and can also encourage others to try:

Jenny is a mentally challenged student who takes private dance lessons every other week. Formerly she took lessons at the studio, with whoever was on duty. She was a little too serious with instructors until one day she met a different instructor who made her laugh all the time. Jenny was able to be more herself with this new instructor; it seemed as if they were meant to work together. The instructor would spend 5 to 10 minutes communicating with her before or during the lesson, so that they became more acquainted, and this helped her to dance more relaxed. After the instructor worked for several weeks with Jenny, she became more at ease and had more fun. For Jenny's sake, she was changed to a weekly private lesson, where she could work with that instruc-

tor and become friends with him. Today, Jenny is a healthier person and a more advanced dancer because she has improved her muscular and mental coordination.

Students with Learning Disabilities

It is not always immediately apparent that special handling is needed for a student with a learning disability. These disabilities are often more subtle than physical or some mental disabilities. It is important that the teacher be alert to the needs of these students, who may not even be aware of the difficulties themselves.

The following case studies illustrate the point of learning disabilities:

An instructor shows Nora some steps, but she has difficulty learning. The instructor can show her the steps and explain them to her, but she still does not get it. She is seriously nearsighted but hates to wear glasses. However, she does not realize that wearing her glasses would improve her vision and perception, so she could learn to dance more easily. Even when she is wearing her glasses, she has difficulty focusing on what she knows and what she is being told.

Nora not only has trouble getting information through her ears and body, she has problems understanding. Her eyes send an image to her brain, but her brain does not recognize the image accurately. She would do fine dancing if that were her only problem, but she also has a poor memory. Only after practicing several times she is able to learn a step. Furthermore, as soon as the instructor moves on to the next step, she has forgotten the first part and must start again as if she has never seen the step before. "Give me some time," her brain says, "to figure out this picture, and see what it reminds me of." So instructors repeat the step for her. Repetition would help if the step or movement were repeated an embarrassing number of times, but, by the time she figures it out, she has forgotten the first part!

*

Lisa has the same problem but is able to cope with this in her everyday life. She uses aids that work for both recognition and memory, such as talking to herself when she observes something. "This is a red and green chair with a high back next to a cushion sofa", she says to herself. This is a cumbersome way to learn to dance. She relies more on following her partner than knowing the steps and, luckily, she is skilled in that area. Her body can almost learn by itself. If she is positioned behind someone while learning how to dance, her body is there, but not her abstract brain. She learns from imitating the dance movement, completely bypassing the analytical part of the brain. This kind of repetition of dance steps helps, because her body has good muscle memory, even though the visual part of her brain does not.

*

When Lola dances the mambo, her visual brain cannot interpret or produce body movement, because of her level of interest. Lola is taking dance lessons because of her partner Richard. Her level of interest is low, and therefore her body may not respond as well. The physical body usually responds to the person's desire, which if absent, in turn becomes a disability.

Here is an example of a common disability as it relates to music:

Orlando and Nelly are not disabled, but they have special problems. They are too shy to dance with others in group classes This prevents them from learning normally in a dance class. Sometimes these problems can influence their style of dance.

Also Orlando has no sense of rhythm. Perhaps he has no sense of identical-time periods. In other words, he cannot tell that the spaces between eight-quarter notes are all the same timing.

How does the human brain measure time? Perhaps it is a skill that is built in so well that our brains are born to be just as individualized as our bodies. It is a feeling.

Orlando may also take a long time to notice loud noises when he is buried in soft noises. Does he have a hearing problem? Does he notice a syncopated beat? For him, the important noises are no different from the unimportant noises. It is not because his brain does not hear them, but because his brain never learned that some sounds are more important than others. Orlando needs to learn that some strong beats are more important than others.

Finally, maybe the part of his brain that processes sounds can understand rhythm, but it cannot communicate well with his body. If he were dancing at a club with flashing lights, it would drive him crazy, sending conflicting information. One of the most difficult problems in dancing is the sense of rhythm, a necessity and not an option in dancing, unless one is free to dance without a partner. For Orlando who loves dancing, dancing without a partner might be the easiest solution. Since partner dancing is what his soul cries for, however, Nelly suggests that the instructor concentrate first on teaching steps and then work on the need for rhythm, separating the two. The instructor suggests finding a computer program that has a musical rhythm to which Orlando must respond. The computer might play a Mambo while lights flash to the beat. He would be required to tap the mouse with his foot at every light flash. However, he might prefer to place the mouse on the floor, since the ultimate goal is dancing and not playing piano. In time the program would come closer to the needs of dancing by removing the lights and clicking the mouse only to the rhythm cue. The instructor recommends using flashing lights only in the original Mambo. The program can be in a game format; immediately buzzing when he is wrong and adding points when he is right. After mastering one kind of dance rhythm, the program ought to offer a new one. At another level, he would be required to respond only to the strong beats.

For a learning disabled student to learn steps and technique, much depends on the ingenuity and interest of the instructor. Much also depends on how often the student practices and how serious his/her disability is.

Physically Challenged Students

If you want to be a dancer but have only one arm or hand, it may not be as difficult to learn as you think. You can always learn ballroom dancing in free style form. You do not need to hold hands with your partner or instructor, but you do need to learn the steps. Later, with any fast dances like hustle, swing or cha-cha you can use one hand to lead or follow your partner in a closed or open position.

Doing slow dances can sometimes be more challenging but not impossible, because it requires that you lead or follow your partner. For example, if you have only one arm it can be easy to dance with your partner in closed position while doing Waltz, Foxtrot, or Rumba. Learning to dance in a closed position through a diaphragm lead (body contact from the solar plexus) can be more effective in dancing with your partner. A verbal lead can also help your partner follow you until the two of you become physically more acquainted.

Blind Students

Nature is wonderful because it does not discriminate against anyone or anything, but protects everybody and everything.

For example, if you were born blind or have become blind, your soul automatically replaces the blindness with a heightened sense of smell, taste, hearing, touch and extra perception or intuition. The ability of the blind cannot be underestimated, because you may still perceive your partner's intentions or emotions on the dance floor. You are spiritually in touch with yourself more than normal people are and have developed other senses more fully, so you are more aware of sound, feeling, movements, and touch. This heightened intuition can help you respond to others.

Learning to dance through private or group lessons may not be too difficult for you because you can hold your instructor's shoulders while practicing. You can also receive some verbal indications. Whether you lead or follow, you *can* learn to dance. It may be wiser to dance with your instructor because he/she can help you improve and can watch out for others around you at the same time. If you have a blind partner who wants to learn how to dance, this is the time for you to enjoy dancing together. If you know blind people a couple who want to learn to dance, encourage them. A helper may be needed to watch out for them and to help avoid collisions.

PART III
ENSURING AN OPTIMAL EXPERIENCE

Wisdom that is experienced can lead you to happiness.
***

You cannot trust your partner if you do not know him/her.
***

Simplicity leads to less work and questions.
***

Remind others in order to remind yourself.
***

Peace is achieved through wisdom.
***

6

Chapter 6 Practicing

There are several ways to promote enjoyment and help yourself relax while you are learning how to dance:

- Communicating well.
- Relaxing physically.
- Taking a positive attitude toward practicing.

Choosing a Place to Practice

If you like to go to crowded places to dance, you are naturally a "people person" and need to be around others for interaction. Through others you can also learn about yourself and about your dancing. You may lose interest in places where there are not many opportunities to socialize, and you may feel more comfortable if you can enjoy the evening with a variety of people. However, you may prefer to go to places which are less crowded so you and your partner can more effectively practice your dancing.

Communicating on the Dance Floor

The ultimate goal for couples is to find the spiritual, emotional, physical or intellectual connection that will allow them to move together and to experience the joy of moving to the music. The more charming both of you look on the dance floor, the more comfortable and advanced you will look. Making each other look good and having fun is what dancing is all about.

One of the most important elements of dancing is, of course, the communication of a leader. A clear lead can make the woman feel more relaxed and move easily. It requires a great deal of upper body control and flexibility on the leader's part and an assertive personality; it is necessary to guide the woman firmly without being too strong or too rough. Eye contact is a very important aspect in dancing because it can help both men and women lead and follow more effectively. They do not need to stare into each other's eyes, but to look for the hints in body movement as an important part of the lead. This makes it easier for the woman to anticipate or be more receptive to the next movement. For example, when the man raises his left arm up, it is understood that the woman is supposed to turn under clockwise or counterclockwise, depending on the lead.

If you are a man, pay attention to your partner's body movements while dancing, so that you can lead her more effectively. Be aware of how your partner responds to your lead and make adjustments to improve it. As a man, it is your responsibility to make the woman "look good" on the dance floor. Here are the following reminders:

- Give her physical support.
- Make eye contact.
- Provide a firm lead to make dancing more communicative.
- Be humorous so she can relax.
- Wait for her to complete her step before starting another one.

If you are a woman, pay attention to your partner's lead and establish eye contact for a solid connection. It is surprising how much unspoken communication takes place through people's eye contact on and off the dance floor. However, if you have difficulty looking straight into your partner's eyes, you may be more comfortable looking at his/her chin or upper body.

If you have difficulty leading your partner in crowded places or are reacting to those who are dancing next to you, this may be because you have difficulty interacting with others, may be antisocial or easily distracted. If you find yourself feeling uncomfortable because of other dancers around you or worrying that others are going to harm you by stepping on your feet, you may interact more comfortably in much less crowded places.

You do not have to know many steps or dances to look good and have a good time with your partner, because with the simplest steps you can create a masterpiece if you execute them with confidence, smoothness and pleasure. Sensual, gentle movements can be incorporated into ballroom dances such as the Latin dances, Swing, and Hustle. Argentine Tango is also a very sensual dance, enabling you through embellishments to express your individuality. Both Argentine Tango and Lambada, for instance, enable dancers to express their sensuality with their partners.

Sometimes you will want to focus on developing your dancing technique, but other times you will simply want to improvise and enjoy dancing with your partner. At such times, you should not have to concentrate too much or think about how you look on the dance floor. Verbal communication can be helpful while improvising with someone new, and communicating with your partner while dancing can make both of you more relaxed and comfortable.

Constant repetition of dances you are practicing can help develop confidence and assertiveness. However, too strong an ego on and off the dance floor does not necessarily mean that you have a positive self-image. If you find yourself constantly showing off on the dance floor, it raises the question of why you want people to look at you. Are you looking for recognition, attention or simply want to prove yourself? Enjoy yourself and your partner naturally, and people will enjoy watching the two of you dancing. Later, as you become more confident of your dancing, you can begin to ask more advanced dancers to dance with you. This will help you learn more steps and style.

Inviting Others to Dance

Inviting others to dance can help you develop self-confidence, because you can learn to take the initiative regardless of rejection.

- If you are a woman, it is often easier for you to ask men to dance, especially if you are a good dancer. It is also important if you are a beginner dancer, not to be intimidated when a good dancer asks you to dance, especially if you do not know them. In fact this can be an opportunity to improve yourself on the dance floor as well as to interact with advanced dancers. Do not worry what the other person is thinking, feeling or expecting of your dancing, just enjoy.
- If you are a man, you may have a difficult time asking women who are good dancers to dance. You may be shy and not know how to approach them. To ask a woman to dance, you should simply greet her and invite her. If she rejects you, she may be tired or not like the music, so you can try again later. If she refuses a second time, you should move on to the next person until you find a partner who will enjoy dancing with you.

- Asking someone to dance merely because they are attractive can backfire. You may have thought you wanted to dance with them, but find out that there is neither connection nor chemistry between you to help you enjoy your dancing. It begins to feel awkward because the two of you have very different personalities and later you may feel disappointed. Therefore, do not let your eye alone make decisions for you on the dance floor. Listen to your feelings. Then, decide if you want to dance with that person.

Reacting to Compliments

When you receive a compliment from a partner about your dancing, interpret the compliment on the basis of your partner's understanding and experience of dance. For example:

- If your partner dances as well as you do, he/she knows what to look for, such as your ability to respond spontaneously to the music, and your technique and style.
- If your partner is a beginning level student, the compliment may be only an indication that he/she cannot do all the things you do. Although your partner may not understand the technical aspects and the styling, he/she is impressed.
- If your partner is very experienced or a professional, the compliment tells you that you are a good dancer because of your feeling, technique, and style.
- If your partner has improved his/her dancing and gives you a compliment for the first time, this is a good sign of his/her own improvement. Even though you may have been dancing much longer than your partner, he/she is beginning to appreciate and understand what you are doing on the dance floor.

The following suggestions will help you relax more in dance situations:

- Dance with your eyes closed when you need to help yourself relax and get in touch with the music and your muscle memory. Closing your eyes while dancing and enjoying your music can be very fulfilling. With practice you can become more in tune with yourself, the music and your partner. This is because with your eyes closed you must rely only on your touch and your sixth sense.
- Breathe in through the nostrils and out through the mouth while dancing. This can help you to relax and absorb more oxygen into the body. Beginning students who are learning new steps may forget to breathe while learning to dance, making their body become tense and sweaty.
- As you breathe out, keep your mouth slightly open. This can give you a more relaxed appearance while dancing.
- Leave your watch at home. Do not worry about time while you are out dancing and having fun with your friends. Learn to enjoy the moment. Becoming constantly aware of the time will only remind you of your basic routines and restrictions.

Adding Yourself to the Equation

Dance is the expression of your soul, mind, body and emotions. Nothing is required but desire, feeling, passion, free movements, and non verbal communication, because the music can put you into a trance-like state. However, if you become a competitive dancer you will need to learn communication, feeling, balance, timing, coordination, posture, momentum, and the rhythm, tempo, and melody of the music.

Few are the instructors and dance studios that understand all these aspects of dancing well enough that they can teach you both the foundation of dance and the expressive aspect of it. Teaching you the steps may not be enough, because this does not prepare you to communicate with your partners on different levels or on different dance floors. Dancing is triggered by music and emotions both within and without.

Learning the footwork, steps or the mechanics may be enough if you are a beginner. Later you may learn the style, technique, and the personality of the dance. Men in particular may enjoy intellectualizing and becoming more familiar with their routines. In contrast, women enjoy and experience their feelings, which are more valuable than just intellectualizing the dance routines. Knowledge is conceptual, while feeling is experiential and enjoyable, and if you become in touch with your feelings you can become a true dancer since feelings are the language or inner voice of your spirit.

For example, when American Indians do the sun dance, they go into a trance, and disconnect themselves from the outside world. They are absorbed by the mystical energies within and without, and are subconsciously transported to other dimensions, as in dreams.

People experience their past, present, and future (body, mind and spirit) because these three stages exist in the present moment. For instance, your physical body holds your past ideas about yourself, your mind holds your present, and your soul holds your future. You can experience all of these in the present moment.

The following is one of my experiences going into a trance through music while dancing:

In 1987, I was out with friends at a night club doing freestyle dancing with someone, and I was having such a good time, I felt that the music was getting into my skin and my soul. Suddenly, as the DJ played my favorite song, I felt transported into another world, suspended in the air with different colored lights around me. It felt wonderful. When I came back to my senses at the nightclub, the song was almost finishing, and I realized that I had been in two places at the same time. I had not been aware of my physical body or other physical things, but my soul was vibrating and floating in the sky. My partner even told me that I had appeared lost somewhere else while I was dancing with her.

Becoming Ready for Success

Defining success:

- Success is when you consciously choose something you love to do and become good at it without having undue stress, no matter what it is. Success is not how much money you make, but whether you achieve peace of mind in your life.
- When you become mentally ready for success, you will understand how not to make decisions with your head (what is convenient for you), but with your heart, and not to be judgmental of yourself or others. In addition, being optimistic can give you inner strength to find solutions for everything.
- When you become physically ready for success, you will start taking care of yourself by dancing or exercising, maintaining a healthy diet, and encouraging others to do the same.

- Finally, the very important aspect of success in dancing is to become spiritually ready. In other words, act before you think. The acting comes from your feelings or your soul, while the thinking comes from your analytical mind. You will be wiser if you stay out of your mind and become more in touch with your feelings.
- Believing in abundance in life can help you avoid destructive competition with others. Additionally, if you define success based on how much money you have then you are in the wrong business, because it will impose great limitations and expectations on yourself and others.
- Choosing to teach dancing can be challenging because it requires you to be emotionally, mentally, physically, and spiritually ready if you want to achieve success. In other words, dealing with deep emotions that can come out in different individuals can be difficult for immature instructors.

There is no failure in life, only more experience.
***

If you do not feel special, you are going to ask your partner how special you are to him/her.
***

Look to your past to make your present wiser and healthier.
***

The way you love yourself,
is the way you experience the love of others.
***

You are what you think, say, and do.
***

We are all one.
***

7

Chapter 7 Etiquette for Dancers

Basic Suggestions

Good manners are very important in our society, in the dance environment as well as in your personal life. The attitude you portray affects how others perceive you. Good manners can improve your relations with others and help you attract more partners and students. Here are some ideas on how to improve your manners in dance-related situations:

- Always say "thank you" after you have danced with someone.
- Compliment other people's dancing when you like it.
- Never interrupt or cut in when two people are having fun on the dance floor.
- Introduce yourself before dancing if you do not know your partner.
- Be polite when someone rejects your invitation to dance.
- Never leave without saying goodbye to the host or hostess of the private party you are attending.

Separateness creates indifference, which makes it harder to help others or for others to help you. However, unity creates compassion, which enables you to help each other and develop strength within.

Becoming Healthier in Your Dance Environment

- If you find yourself disappointed with your dance partner it is often because of your expectations–have more faith and keep helping him/her.
- If you react negatively while dancing with a partner who is less advanced than you, it is because of your repressed anger or fear. Try to be more patient and understanding of your partner's dance level.
- If you experience physical or mental pain it is because of your judgments of yourself and others. Remove the judgment and the pain will disappear (do not confuse judgment with observation. Judgment is when you condemn and assume how you feel about others without knowing them, while observation is what you see and know about others behaviors and feelings).
- If your partner criticizes and complains too much, he/she is in pain. This attitude can eventually affects you. Find another partner.
- If you worry about what your partner is doing, thinking, expecting, wanting or feeling, it is because you are feeling insecure. Simply stay in the moment, or enjoy yourself dancing with other people.
- If you are too hard on yourself or on others, it is because you are a perfectionist. Be gentle and kind because it is your nature.
- If you find yourself working too hard in your dance relationship, it is because you are not being yourself. The more you know yourself, the more you can be yourself.

- If you are an open-minded dancer, you are naturally more willing to change your perceptions and grow up in life as well as in your dancing.
- If you socialize with others who are positive and healthy, it can help you to bring out your own positive and healthy attitude.
- If you appreciate yourself, you will need less recognition from others.
- If you analyze the outside world too much, you will hold your inner world back from evolving–try to observe the outside world without judgments.

Some Practical Reminders

- Be aware of your dance body language.
- Try to have fun even when you are working hard in your dancing.
- Maintain light resistance through the hands and arms.
- Make eye contact with your partner.
- Play some modern music to dance ballroom dances to inspire you differently.
- Practice ballroom dancing as freestyle.
- Relax and hold back your shoulders.
- Stay semi-close to your partner.
- Try different teachers to improve and bring out different facets of yourself.
- Wear comfortable shoes and clothing.
- Use easy breathing, in through the nose and out through the mouth.

Becoming a Friend with your Partner

Becoming a friend with your partner can be a powerful tool in helping each other:

- Know your partner, so you can help him/her to be more of him/herself on and off the dance floor.
- Use your partner's dance talents, so you can become a more advanced dancer than you were before.
- Trust your partner so you can love him/her, because you cannot love what you do not trust.
- Help your partner so you can help yourself, because you and your partner are one.
- Practice with your partner at least twice a week so you can create unity.
- Do not let your ego create separateness because you are not superior or inferior to anybody, you are just different and special like everybody else.

Negative Vibes

If you are a romantic, happy, and passionate dancer and find yourself feeling negative vibes while dancing with a partner, you may be perceiving negative thoughts from that person, or somebody else is sending you negative thoughts. Perhaps your dance partner is going through hard times and is not aware that he/she is projecting negative vibes, which are triggering your own negative repressed emotions. The more you care for yourself, the healthier partner you will attract.

Moody Dancers

If you have a tendency to be moody while interacting with others on and off the dance floor, you may be reacting to your unsuccessful and unresolved past experiences with others. In other words, you are still in pain and bitter about your past experiences, and now you are reacting to your new experiences by emotionally or psychologically protecting yourself.

Conflicts on the Dance Floor

Many dancers wonder why they feel and behave differently dancing with different partners. It is because of the personal chemistry (similar thought patterns) you release while interacting or dancing with others. For example, when you and your partner both have domineering personalities, there may be a struggle for power or control on the dance floor. In fact, if you have a strong ego, you may fight for territory on the dance floor to prove your talent to your partner. During this kind of conflict, your partner may take some control for a while and then you may fight back. When two angry people are dancing together they will trigger and feed each other's anger. It is wise to change partners.

When two passive dancers are on the dance floor, they may not create enough spark to enhance their dancing, because neither one triggers the other one's assertiveness or passion. Assertive dancers can easily trigger passive people to become more outgoing on the dance floor by bringing out their repressed assertiveness. On the other hand, passive dancers can make hyper people slow down on the dance floor and even in their personal lives because they are attracting what they need, and that is to slow down.

Many believe that personality conflicts on the dance floor are normal for the process of couples working out their relationships. Yet if they lack self-knowledge how can they understand their partners' problems in order to make the dancing or the relationship healthier? (if you do not understand a problem, you cannot solve it). In this society, men are characterized by Mars and women by Venus, total opposites. In reality, these stereotypes may not apply to either one; this attitude only creates separateness rather than unity. Men and women have both right and left brain characteristics, but they express themselves differently. The problem is that because of their environment, most men have repressed some of their right-brain characteristics (acceptance, sensitivity, freedom), which make it harder to understand women. Women on the other hand, often understand men more because they are naturally more receptive or intuitive.

Becoming Aroused

If you suddenly become aroused for no apparent reason while dancing with your partner, it may be because your partner or someone else may be thinking about you sexually and sending out these thoughts. You in turn are receiving them and reacting by becoming aroused on or off the dance floor. When you are sexually attracted to someone, you are unconsciously projecting your thoughts and desires to that person while dancing. You are always sending thoughts or energy out into the world about yourself, and often to those who have similar thought patterns. Furthermore, when you and your partner have similar sexual ideas about each other (like attracts like), the attraction begins to take place.

This can happen anywhere, at any distance, especially if you are a sensitive person. These thoughts often trigger your sexuality and you become aroused. If you experience this with your partner or student while dancing, you may fall in love or in lust. You may end up pursuing your partner for more excitement until he/she gives in. You can however, always restrict this physical pleasure and attention to the dance floor if you do not want to exchange this sexual energy.

Falling in Love with an Instructor

Defining love:
Love is giving and receiving unconditionally. Accepting yourself for who you are allows you to accept others for who they are. If you want to experience the grandest love, you have

to give yourself emotionally, physically, mentally, and spiritually to yourself and your partner without hidden agendas so your partner may do the same. If you want to have everything, you have to give up everything. Therefore, the way you love yourself is the way you are going to experience the love of others because what you project, you also attract. If you do not love yourself, you will have the tendency to ask your partner how much he/she loves you. In other words, you are validating that you do not love yourself or do not know how to and therefore you will be looking for others to love you. However, when you love yourself there is no need to ask your partner how much he/she loves you, because you know that you are love and you just want to share it. When you feel insecure about yourself, you are going to feel insecure about your partner, even though your partner may not feel insecure about you.

Do not confuse love with need. When you *love* your partner, you love him/her freely for who he/she is without requirements or expectations; if your partner leaves you, you still love him/her. When you *need* your partner, it is when you think you love him/her because of what he/she has done for you, and therefore, you will have a hard time leaving your partner.

Being or falling in love is when someone makes you aware by triggering the love within yourself (turning on the light within you). In other words, this love or feeling that has been dormant, suddenly wakes up and begins to appreciate life and the one who triggered the love. Unfortunately, when your mind becomes aware of this love it begins to create a scenario and expectations of yourself and your partner that eventually may make you fall out of love rather than experience and share this unconditional feeling in every present moment. Therefore, you do not need to look for love or relationships, because you *are* love, you just need to turn on the light within you and demonstrate with the one you are attracting. There always will be someone who will trigger the love within you sooner or later because you need to be reminded of who you really are.

The following are other reasons why you may think you have fallen in love with your instructor or with your ideas about her/him:

- You like his/her personality.
- You find him/her sexually attractive.
- Your instructor may be a parental role-model.
- You are attracted to good dancers.

It is inevitable that you project your own personal chemistry (ideas about yourself), and those who teach you to dance may unconsciously or consciously perceive your thoughts or intentions, and may in turn return your feelings.

You may fall in love with the person from whom you are taking lessons because of the strong chemistry between the two of you, because you are receiving emotional support and becoming friends or because she/he is a wonderful person to be around. Your needs and ideas may develop from wanting to be like those who are teaching you, and this can be an opportunity for you to become what you may be holding back.

If such an attraction occurs, it helps to know why you feel so attracted to the person who is teaching you. Whether you are single or married, this attraction allows you to experience and feel some kind of enjoyment. The intrigue and taboo sometimes can challenge both to have a taste for more physical contact when dancing, and if you do not control your desires, (desire is the first step in creation) you may embark on a love affair.

Another reason you may like your instructor is that he/she is physically attractive and confident, so you fall in love with your idea of him/her, rather than with the real person underneath. Your instructor, who dances very well, is considered very attractive and is much sought after. The idea of your instructor being in such demand could be appealing to you, and this may be a reason you like to be with him/her.

An affair between instructors and students who are physically attracted to each other or those who think alike occurs more frequently than people realize. An affair usually starts when student and teacher each like the other's looks and personality. When a student also enjoys the instructor's dancing, they become closer friends or lovers. Married women who are domineering and assertive toward their husbands may enjoy having an instructor with a strong personality who can dominate them on the dance floor. Many single instructors who are great entertainers may go through several love affairs because of the opportunities they created, and because they enjoy making others happy. Therefore, when students find happiness with some physical and emotional support and pleasure, they may experience a love affair.

If you have been taking dance lessons for several years from single instructors and suddenly get married, you may feel you must stop taking lessons because you no longer have the same freedom to become affectionate or intimate on the dance floor. Many students become physically and emotionally attached to their instructors, and after marriage, they must transfer that attachment. This may be an indication that the students initially had different intentions for the dance lessons, such as dating the instructor, having an affair, or just seeking physical and emotional support.

Sexual Harassment

In the dance environment, sexual harassment is a controversial topic. Both students and instructors can be responsible for sexual harassment. Therefore, there are not victims or villains in life only creators who unconsciously or consciously create situations where sexual harassment occurs.

You may be sexually harassed by your instructor or your student not because you are being a victim, but because you are attracting or calling upon this experience. The two of you have created this situation, or perhaps you are needing sexual attention and your aggressor is perceiving this.

It may be easier for a woman to sexually harass a male instructor than for a male student to harass a female instructor, because men are generally more vulnerable or open to sex. Women are sexually and emotionally more conservative and choose their partners carefully because they listen to their feelings; most men listen to their mind. Although, men and women are equally sexual, women tend to be more discreet than men.

Some women may lead on their dance instructors to get free private lessons outside their dance studios. If you become aware that your instructor is turned on by you, you may think that this can be an opportunity to take advantage of this. You may start out by being friendly, charming, and later teasing your instructor, to see how he/she will respond or react. If your instructor responds in a physical manner, such as by having more body contact with you while dancing he/she may be giving you the green light. However, if your instructor responds negatively, it is an indication that he/she wants only your business. Most male instructors have a hard time fighting these temptations from women, because they may enjoy feeding their egos.

The following may contribute to sexual harassment:

- If you fear negative things about your sexuality you may experience them, because what you send out, you also attract (law of attraction).

- Being sexually molested in your childhood may also contribute to sexual harassment because the trauma has created a continuous fear that you inevitably project, which in turn may attract similar experiences (what you fear you will call upon).
- Being lonely can make you repress your sexuality, which in turn triggers your sexuality by others and can cause you to react forcefully.
- Needing love and attention allows you to put your guard down, thus allowing others to take advantage of you.

Sexual harassment or unasked for sexual attention by your instructor may be created unconsciously or consciously by both you and your aggressor. You may not realize that you are sexually needy and may have brought on this attention unwittingly. However, it is never appropriate for any instructor to take advantage of a student unless there is complete mutual consent between the two adults. Taking advantage of students who are minors is, under no circumstances to be tolerated.

Here are some experiences of sexual harassment in the dance environment:

Kenny loves to go out to different nightclubs to dance and to have a good time with his friends. He dances with different women, but there is one in particular that he likes. One day while dancing the waltz with this particular woman, he suddenly became sexually aroused for no apparent reason. He wondered why this was happening, because he was not thinking of her sexually. He decided to ask her whether or not she was thinking about him while they were dancing. She admitted that she indeed had been fantasizing about him while they were waltzing, because she felt physically attracted to him. He began to understand that something in his partner's thoughts and desires was triggering his own sexual arousal.

*

"*I was wondering why I was having sexual dreams about one of my female friends. I decided to talk to her the next time I had one of my dreams. When I had a sexual dream about her, I called her the next day and asked whether she had been thinking about me sexually. When she admitted she had, I immediately said: "That's okay, I was just wondering, because last night I had a sexual dream about you and I didn't know what to think of it." Originally I had felt that she was intruding on my privacy, but I now understand more deeply how thoughts can travel and be received as a message through dreams".*

*

"*My partner and I went to a dance studio to take a few private lessons in Tango from a male instructor, and after the third lesson my instructor began pressing my breasts against his chest in a suggestive manner. I thought it was part of the dance position–that two people were suppose to be close, but he continued to press my breasts against his chest and I began to feel uncomfortable. Later, he offered me a free one-on-one Tango lesson, while my partner was standing off to the side waiting to dance with me. During the lessons, my instructor was still paying too much attention to me and very little to my partner, until my partner realized that this instructor was sexually harassing me. My partner and I left the studio without even finishing our package of private lessons.*"

*

"*After being indulged with magical moments, I experienced sexual harassment in the dance world.*

Maybe I have just been spoiled by being able to feel free and uninhibited, because of the trust I have had with each and every dance instructor I have worked with. That all changed when some sexual remarks and advances were made while I was dancing with a male instructor. I assumed that from one professional to another (I am a dance instructor myself), I would be treated with respect–my mistake! I am unaccustomed to putting my guard up, because it takes away from the joy I normally experience when I dance. I am usually a very perceptive person and have been known to be standoffish when the need arises. I had known this particular teacher, so I was caught off guard when the gestures were made. Throughout the years, both physical contact and verbal remarks about parts of my anatomy have been made by different dance instructors. The difference is that they were made in a constructive way (and in front of my classmates). I am sure that I was always unconsciously aware that I had no sexual worries with my gay instructors; for instance. I always relaxed when dancing or performing with them. As for my heterosexual instructors, their body language was and is their most evident form of communication with me. When an instructor makes a sexual remark or dance movement, I feel an interruption of the fluid motion I love to experience when I dance! The only thing I know to do is let my feelings of revulsion be known, and remove myself from the situation, which I have done.

*

"After my last experience with an instructor, I was not sure I wanted to continue. My friend Silvia and I wanted to learn the salsa, so we signed up for ten private lessons. From the first lesson we had prob-

lems. First, the instructor did not teach us the Salsa as we had asked him to. He started showing us the samba, and we frequently had to ask him to stay focused on salsa. Second, we soon realized that private lessons did not actually mean what we thought it meant, that is, Silvia and me together with him alone. He had at least one and sometimes two other students in the room that he was helping at the same time. However, the worse part was when the instructor began placing his hands frequently and inappropriately close to Silvia's breast. We learned by watching other lessons that he did this with all the women. I was also angered to learn that he had made a pass at Silvia at the first lesson, saying how much he wanted to teach her the Tango. We were disappointed with the experience and felt like we had wasted our money."

Preventing Sexual Harassment

You cannot prevent what you already have unconsciously or consciously created, but a change of mind and behavior can help you to change your experience. Beingness creates everything you experience in life. For example, when you are being sexual you are calling upon the experience. This is certainly not to imply that women or men are consciously asking to be sexually harassed. However, unconscious thoughts are powerful suggestions that can trigger the aggressor to act and harass those of similar thought patterns. The following are ways of dealing with such situations:

- Speak out to your instructor and change your behavior toward him/her, or choose another instructor.

- Try not to schedule a private lesson when you and your instructor are alone in the studio or a house, or make sure there are other people practicing or teaching dancing in the same room.

- If you feel or perceive your instructor's sexual intentions while dancing, discreetly but firmly push him away. It is always up to you to say no or simply enjoy the attention without going any further.

- If you and your partner are taking private lessons, suggest that your instructor spend equal time with each of you.

- You can dance in an open position to avoid body contact or sexual harassment, but this position may require more upper body resistance to follow or lead your partner. Some instructors may like to teach leading or following through diaphragm contact, so you can communicate with your partner more effectively, but this can be an option if you are not comfortable with a particular individual.

Reputation

The reputation of an instructor can be very important in the dance business, because it can give him/her either glory or hard times. A good reputation shows honesty, punctuality, sensitivity, friendship, good intentions, ethics, and respect for students' free will. In addition, a good reputation can create financial success, because an instructor with a good reputation usually believes in abundance and is more psychologically, emotionally and spiritually prepared to handle it.

However, having a negative reputation may reduce an instructor's business, as well as create enemies and isolation from the rest of the dance community. If the instructor becomes financially successful from cheating others by making them sign big contracts and giving them inexperienced instructors, his business may eventually collapse.

Making Enemies

Jealousy, anger, selfishness, ignorance, and a competitive attitude can lead you to self-destruction. This is not the way to function with instructors or other students: everyone loses opportunities to get ahead and become successful dancers. Successful instructors are not necessarily those who have a lot of money or many students, but those who help others to become happy and joyful dancers. Feeling happy, joyful, having peace of mind, being free of undue stress, and being honest are all part of success.

Here is an experience from a dance instructor name George:

I have been teaching ballroom dancing for several years, and it can be a very competitive business among instructors and students, but I just do my work by teaching, giving people what they need and want, and being straightforward. However, one day I found out another instructor was talking behind my back, saying that I was domineering, jealous, possessive and a playboy. Because of his remarks, new students began to wonder about me. There was nothing I could do about it until my students got to know me more and form their own ideas about me. I knew the other instructor was jealous, because I have always had more attention from female students and also had a successful business. One day I decided to confront him and tell him to stop saying negative things about me to other people, but he denied ever having said them. Later, he did it again, and we got into a physical fight. We began avoiding each other at social dances, but I had no peace of mind until a few months later, when we started to talk again and become more acquainted; eventually we began to accept and respect each other.

                            *

I was a full-time dance instructor at a dance studio. My students used to bring me gifts every time they went on vacation, because I gave them good dance lessons and good times. However, other instructors started noticing and wondering about me. I could not help having fun with my students: entertaining, singing, humoring, and sometimes teaching a little too much, until some instructors became jealous and began complaining to the manager. After a few weeks, the manager cut me back to part-time because I was not selling enough dance lessons–a good excuse to lay me off. Apparently my students were talented and learned the bronze level very quickly, so I started teaching them the more advanced bronze level. Later, the manager fired me because he thought that I was doing something wrong by teaching them so rapidly. My students were disappointed when the manager gave them a different instructor, telling them that I went to work for another studio. Students become attached to their instructors, so, when they are assigned several instructors a year, they get annoyed and begin to wonder whether there is something wrong with the studio's policies, especially if they do not see their instructors any more.

Friction with Your Instructor

Because you are paying money for your lessons, the instructor has to hold his/her temper or repress his/her emotions when there is friction between the two of you. Furthermore, you have the advantage if you become angry with your instructor, because you know that he/she has to avoid making you angry or you might stop the lessons. However, if your instructor is a person who likes to keep things smooth with you and other students, he/she will not hesitate to stop teaching you if you become too pushy or give him/her a hard time. An instructor however, should treat you the same as other students, and should show respect and patience. A good relationship with each other makes learning more enjoyable and successful.

You can only define yourself through your own actions.

***

Romance can be joyfully expressed through dancing.

***

You cannot experience what you do not know.

***

Nothing is new, you are rediscovering today what you have forgotten in the past.

***

All insecurities are illusions, avoid them.

***

Possession becomes an obsession.

***

8

Chapter 8 Finding a Regular Partner

As you continue to improve, you may want to have a regular partner to dance with. This is not strictly necessary, but it does enable you to focus on steps and routines that interest both of you. Be sure to continue to dance with other people, though, so you can maintain your skills at following and leading.

Places to Look for a Partner

There are many healthy avenues for meeting new partners. The following opportunities would be the most likely to put you in contact with prospective ones:

- Dance group classes and social events.
- Social dance parties on weekdays or weekends, sponsored by many dance studios or by freelance instructors, and at some restaurants where you can have fun meeting new people. See the Internet for information.

Avoid the following:

- Going to singles bars or nightclubs to find a partner. This is not a reliable way to find ballroom dance partners because the rooms are so crowded, smoky, and dark. Also, you cannot judge a person's dance ability in such a confined environment.
- Taking just enough dance lessons to meet people of the opposite sex and stopping when you find someone. You will stop improving and may lose your partner in the long run if he/she continues to take dance lessons.
- Taking dance lessons to avoid personal problems. This approach may lead to building up tension until you become a time bomb ready to explode. Later, you may release your anger on others, which creates more problems. By overcoming your conflicts first, you can enjoy dancing much more freely and attract healthier partners. The problem is that many people become attached to pain, because they believe in punishment or evil which they learn from an early age. This attitude makes it even harder to let go of pain. Therefore, if you decide to be happy, then do happy things, do not do happy things in order to be happy because you are going to resent it.

What to Look for in a Partner

Dancers are a cross-section of the population, but their behavior as dancers tends to put them into these categories:

- Emotional dancers allow their emotions to get in their way when making decisions. They are very sensitive individuals and are easily hurt.
- Intellectual dancers like to analyze and conceptualize everything and everyone. They tend to be *mechanical* dancers rather than *feeling* dancers.

- Grounded or not too emotional dancers tend to dance in a practical way without much emotion or feeling. However, they can also enjoy being around feeling or emotional people.
- Optimistic dancers are usually happy and resourceful people. They like to find solutions for everything and they are easy dancers to get along with.
- Pessimistic dancers tend to complain about life or about dancing. They can bring their partners down emotionally.
- Sexy dancers allow themselves to feel and think about their sexuality on and off the dance floor. They are projecting their sexual thoughts through their body language.
- Spiritual dancers allow themselves to connect with their partners by feeling what is beyond the physical. In other words, looks do not matter for them, as much as feeling good with a partner.
- Tough or macho dancers tend to show their fear and perception about themselves and others. They are holding back their gentle nature. Their dance style can make them look stiff on the dance floor. They may think that a gentle style will look too feminine. Showing their gentle side can make them more flexible.
- Gay dancers are among the most talented people in show business and on the dance floor, because they allow themselves to express their gentleness as well as strength and passion in their dancing.
- Heterosexual dancers may allow themselves only to dance with other heterosexuals and thus only experience limited aspects of people. If heterosexual men have an effeminate dance style, it may suggest that they are expressing their right-brain characteristics (the feminine aspect). They can help women, especially tomboys, develop their feminine dance style (left-brain dominant).

Dancers may fit into one or more of these categories. Understanding them may enable you to get the most out of working with them as dance partners or instructors. For example, if you are an emotional dancer, you may choose an intellectual partner or instructor to bring you balance. If you are a pessimistic type of dancer, you may need an optimistic partner or instructor. If you are a grounded or not too emotional type of dancer, you may need an emotional partner or instructor, etc.

Parent-Child Dancing

Going out social dancing with your sons and daughters or just having parties at your own home can be very fulfilling for your family, because it can bring you together and provide fun at the same time. Moreover, dancing with your sons and daughters at the amateur dance competitions can be a lot of fun and can also develop more communication skills between you.

Chemistry

The chemistry between you and your partner can be the most important aspect in dancing because it can bring you more passion and strength on and off the dance floor. Chemistry means similar thought patterns between you and your partner—like attracts like. Without chemistry, it is more difficult to perform or dance freely together. In fact, it may be harder to get along with your partner both in dancing and in your personal life if you are romantically involved. Some people simply 'click' on the dance floor. They communicate without many verbal signals because of the strong chemistry between them. By complimenting each other, flirting, smiling, and having a good time, they communicate and dance well together. When two dancers have similar personalities such as being very physical, playful, optimistic, loving or intellectual, they immediately attract each other. Similarly, a selfish, unhappy, pessimistic, or artistic person will attract those with similar characteristics.

On the other hand, when you and your partner are attracted to each other, but the two of you seem very different, one of you may be repressing part of your personality. Perhaps one of you is humorous, sexual, and intellectual while the other is more serious, less sexual, and unhappy. You are still attracting each other so that each of you can learn more about yourselves. Finding yourself wanting to be intimately or romantically involved with your partner can be difficult if there are no similarities. If you get turned on only by your partner's looks, your partnership may not last too long because it has been only physical. However, becoming friends and getting to know your partner first will allow you to experience more joy together because you will know who she/he is from within.

Finding a compatible partner is not always easy, and if you do find one, it may be temporary because of your having chosen him/her for the wrong reasons or because you had faulty intentions or expectations to begin with. You dream of having the perfect partner: tall, thin, strong, pretty and smart, and that is what your mind looks for. However, you will probably attract something quite different, because of the things you need to learn about yourself through him/her. Every dance partner you had has been the right partner for you at the time, however, because you have attracted him/her as an opportunity to become more aware of yourself.

Healing Your Partner

One of the most powerful tools to make your partner feel good is to transmit your positive attitude. For example, if you perceive that your partner is not feeling healthy or has had a bad day at work or at home, there is a way to heal him/her while dancing. He/she does not even need to know what you are doing. First, observe your partner's symptoms as follows:

- Any kind of rejections.
- Complaining too much about others.
- Feelings of stress or anger.
- Projecting aloofness.
- Wanting to argue.

What you can do for your partner while you are taking a lesson or practicing:

- Become aware of your warm hands and place them on your partner while dancing.
- Embrace your partner with your soul in a loving way.
- Feel consciously good doing it for your partner.
- Feel love for your partner.
- Talk as little as possible.

At the end of the lesson or practice, you will most likely receive a compliment. Your partner will feel healthier and happier.

This can be a comfortable way for anyone to feel safe with you and to be close to you as an instructor, student or partner.

Picture by Xenophon G. Stamoulis

Picture by Xenophon G. Stamoulis

Picture by Kay Lyn

Picture by CIA photographer

Picture by Bruce Parker

Picture by Don Critchfield

Happiness allows you to see beauty in everyone and everything.

***

What you look up disappears because it is an illusion.

***

What you think you need is already there for you.

***

Happiness creates positive circumstances.

***

Before you solve other people's problems, solve your own first.

***

What you resist will indeed persist.

***

9

Chapter 9 Taking Care of Yourself and Avoiding Burnout

Through other activities you can prepare yourself for dancing and avoid burning out.

Your State of Mind

Health is a state of balance within your soul, mind, and body. In other words, when you feel happy and comfortable, it is because you are balanced, just as feeling uncomfortable suggests that you are feeling imbalanced. If you are going through hard times, it may be because you are listening too much to your mind. Do not let your mind control your life.

There are ways you can positively affect your dancing:

- Increasing your level of physical fitness.
- Improving your breathing technique.
- Improving your physical flexibility.
- Increasing your musical sensitivity.

Increasing your Level of Physical Fitness

By doing other sports such as swimming, jogging, yoga, bicycling, basketball or others, you can improve your dancing, because these exercises serve to balance and help your muscle coordination. These sports involve all the major muscles in the body and can give you more overall mental and physical fitness. You can learn to exercise with your hands and feet, improving muscle coordination as you find and feel the rhythm of the music. It is also important that you become aware of your own body movements while exercising, or dancing, because it can bring you more harmony (feeling your partner's rhythm in the present moment).

Too much dancing or exercising, however, to the point of mental or physical pain, can cause you to burn out. Pushing yourself too hard, you may become tolerant to pain and therefore attached to it. If you feel physical or mental discomfort while exercising, stop; meditation and less judgments may help you ease your pain and detach yourself from the outside world. Eating well, thinking positive, and working on your breathing technique can also help you sleep well.

Practicing your dancing without music for a few minutes during class can help you become aware of your own body language, because music can distract you from paying attention to your body movements or perfecting your steps. However, dancing without music for more than 30 minutes during class can be boring, especially if you are a feeling dancer who depends on the music to move or dance.

Increasing your Breathing Technique

Breathing is important in dancing, because it can help you relax, retain more oxygen, and improve your endurance on and off the dance floor. Inhaling through the nose and exhaling through the mouth can help you maintain your energy level without becoming too tired or sweaty. Practice this breathing technique daily to release tension and help you become a stronger dancer. If you breathe slowly it may slow the pumping of the blood to the heart. Shallow breathing, however, may indicate repressed emotions such as sadness, and pity. Holding tightly to these negative emotions may eventually result in lung problems.

Improving your Physical Flexibility

You should consider practicing other types of movements to improve your flexibility and endurance:

- Aerobics
- Ballet
- Jazz
- Modern dance
- Yoga

Experiencing these different dances or exercises can increase your flexibility and versatility in dance movement, and can compliment your ballroom dancing. New dance movements can bring you a deeper connection to different feelings, so that you can express yourself differently.

Increasing your Musical Sensitivity

Learning to play a musical instrument can augment your development as a unique dancer, because you can become more aware of the feeling of the music. This can naturally inspire new dance movements even if they are not in your dance syllabus.

- Playing the drums can help you understand rhythm and allow you to express the tempo of your music.

- Playing the violin can allow you to express your emotions and follow the melody.

If you are a classical musician who plays the guitar or the trumpet, for example, you can easily learn to do slow dances such as Waltz, Foxtrot, Rumba or Tango because you are naturally in touch with the melody and the smoothness of the music. You are able to transfer your feelings effectively to your dance movements.

Singing can also be a wonderful tool to help you retain the melody while dancing. Being a great or professional singer is not necessary, but you can be a gentle and smooth singer while dancing. However, if you are a professional singer, it can help you improve the expressive quality of your body language if you dance while you sing and it may make you more attractive as a performer especially in a rock or Latin band.

Other Ways to Help Yourself Become more Expressive

Being in touch with nature can inspire you and help you improve your dancing. For example, expressing rain by bringing your hands up and shaking your fingers on the way down or a thunderstorm through the snap of your arm, lends drama and passion to your dancing. Imitating animals' body movements can add another element to your dancing such as the motion of birds taking off which can be expressed through your arms and torso lifting.

Your Attitude

Your attitude can make or break your ballroom dancing experience. The following will all have a positive impact:

- A flexible soul, mind, and body.
- High morale.
- Self-confidence.

Developing Self-confidence

One of the most important ways to develop self-confidence is to give yourself an abundance of pleasure, so that you can then give an abundance of pleasure to your partners and others. Enjoy yourself dancing with your partner, feel the music, become creative and improvise. These behaviors can make you feel good, and they are the foundation for self-confidence. *Know* that you are a confident dancer because knowing will lead into the experience, whereas thinking will lead you only to a concept. Becoming confident takes a decision on your part.

Be aware of becoming a dancer, make decisions, and take action. This can lead to a dream come true. In addition, a positive attitude, good diet, and exercise can lead you into a good and healthy life-style.

Learning to become a dance instructor can be one way to achieve self-confidence and take control of your life, because it can help you to create a new identity—dance instructor—in addition to the other things you do.

Incorporate your jazz, ballet, and other dance experience into your ballroom dancing to improve your style and increase your confidence. Repeated practicing of your steps and technique can help you improve quickly. Practicing dancing in front of the mirror is a good start to developing self-esteem, because you can watch your progress and get used to watching yourself and accepting your physique.

However, if you become over-confident or arrogant, you may begin to separate yourself from others. Then, your body language may change and you may start losing your integrity. Remember, appreciating yourself and others is the key to success in dancing. By complimenting others appropriately and using good manners, you can make a good impression and dance with the best dancers. This in turn will enhance your self-confidence.

Spiritual Balance

Spiritual, mental, physical and emotional balance are important in your life as in your dancing because they allow you to express your inner joy and can improve your health and lead you to happiness. As a dancer, your well-being depends not only on dancing and exercising, but also on thinking positively and eating well.

Being emotionally balanced can help you become more aware of yourself and your partner. To achieve spiritual, mental and physical balance, you must first express your natural emotions as follows:

- Expressing your love allows you to accept others for who they really are, and be able to give and receive everything or anything unconditionally. However, if you repress your love, you may become possessive, obsessive, controlling, and physically, mentally and emotionally damaging to yourself and your partner. If you do not know what love is, you cannot experience it. Giving but not receiving is a sign that your ego is getting in the way. When instructors become possessive towards their students making them feel suffocated, students eventually stop taking lessons.
- Expressing your fear allows you to avoid dangerous situations on and off the dance floor. If you repress your fear or think that you are not afraid of anything or anybody, you may develop panic attacks, which in turn may cause you to hurt yourself and others. Some instructors who encourage their students not to fear theater art movements

or lifts, for example, may be encouraging them to take undue physical risks they are not prepared for.

- Expressing your envy allows you to rid yourself of the wish to have what others have that you do not (envy allows you to want to achieve more). However, if you repress your envy, you may become jealous, which in turn may cause you to hurt and separate yourself from others. Some professionals do not allow themselves to express their envy toward other professionals who may be excellent dancers because they are afraid that they are putting themselves down.
- Expressing your anger allows you to rid yourself of your disappointments and expectations of others. If you repress your anger, you will eventually experience rage, which in turn can cause you to seriously hurt yourself and others and cause you to develop heart problems. Some instructors may be afraid to express their anger towards their students because they are afraid of losing them, but at the same time they are repressing it and damaging their own health.
- Expressing your grief allows you to get rid of your sadness. However, if you repress your grief, you may develop depression, which leads you to isolate yourself from others and develop lung problems. If professionals or students allow themselves to express their grief on and off the dance floor, they will be healthier.

Expressing all these emotions allows you to become spiritually, mentally and physically healthy. All mental and physical health problems are caused by your thoughts, your mind, or your personality. Therefore, adopt new ideas if you want to change your life to a healthier one.

Signs of unhealthy dancers:

- If you are a controlling dancer, you tend to be over-protective and afraid of losing your partner or your loved ones. You have not yet learned to love yourself.
- If you are a fearless dancer, you are confrontational towards your partners and others. You have not yet admitted your fears to your loved ones and others.
- If you are a jealous dancer, you may easily dislike others and separate yourself from them. You have not yet admitted your envy to your loved ones and others.
- If you are an angry dancer, you may be emotionally and physically pushy towards your partner on and off the dance floor. You have not yet verbally admitted your pain and disappointments.
- If you are a depressed dancer, you may be having problems communicating with your partner on and off the dance floor. You have not yet learned to admit your inner pain and sadness to your loved ones and others.

If you have polluted your spiritual, mental and physical body with repressed emotions while growing up, it can be harder for you to experience all different levels of enjoyment. A constant battle between your mind and your body may lead to conflicts, which may not allow you to transcend the material world to go into your spiritual world. By observing your movements, listening to your inner voice and your surroundings, you will become more in touch with life.

However, your pain can make it harder to connect with your partner while dancing. How many times have you said "What a horrible day," when it is raining and cloudy or "It is too hot," or "It is too cold"? You fight nature. You do not seem to realize that trees need water, cold weather is the time for introspection and healing, hot weather is the time to play and rejuvenate. Renouncing pain and negative connotations about people or things can lead you to more peace of mind. If dancers understand that the soul is the core of life and that their physical body is just the vehicle to express their desires, they can pay more attention to their inner selves and connect to the universe.

Dealing with Burnout

Burnout can be associated with any extreme mental and physical activity. Some of the following may be causes of burnout for dancers or instructors:

- Entertaining others: If you have the tendency to entertain others too much for recognition and attention you may experience burnout. When you become more appreciative of yourself, you will need less recognition from others.

- Stressing yourself before dance competitions: If you are a student who is doing many different dances with your instructor at a competition or a professional who is performing with many different students, you may experience burnout. Moderation can help you keep yourself in good spirits.

- Teaching too many hours: If you are teaching or practicing dancing more than 30 hours a week you may feel very fatigued. Weekly massage or spiritual healing (energy work) may help you release your tension and stress.

- Listening to the same music: Listening to the same music all the time while practicing your dance routines for dance competitions or performances may lead to boredom. A variety of music such as classical, Jazz or meditation music can give you time off from your dance routine music.

Other Stress

If you are spending too much time concentrating on your expectations, steps, technique, and style, you may not be able to enjoy yourself in the process. Yet the process is as important as the result. Our society imposes so many restrictions that it may be hard for you to relax and feel free to enjoy yourself while learning. Not being aware of this may cause you to hold back from expressing yourself and instead to feel guilty and become angry with yourself for not meeting your own expectations soon enough. However, by following your feelings you can attain great enjoyment in your dancing or life because you will be able to free yourself from fear and many outside restrictions.

The combination of stress, negative emotions, and a poor diet can cause you mental weakness, and later on illness.

- Drinking alcohol can be a depressant because alcohol attacks the nervous system, slowing you down and making you depressed. The reason some dancers drink is because they have repressed the ability to make themselves feel good, and they look for something outside of themselves, like alcohol, to give them joy. As a result of using alcohol, you eat more and become aggressive and more violent, diminishing your self-confidence. Furthermore, the smell of alcohol and your behavior after drinking can turn your partners off.
- Using drugs or smoking cigarettes is a sign of a diminished desire to live life, and also of repressing the ability to make yourself feel good naturally. In other words, you are unconsciously and slowly ending your life (smoking cigarettes can lead to lung, mouth, or throat cancer) because of not knowing yourself spiritually.

- Eating junk food such as potato chips, hot dogs, chocolate, fast food and carbonated sodas may reduce your health, sensitivity, and perception of your dancing because of too many chemicals and preservatives in the food. Drinking water and juices is always healthier than drinking sodas and alcohol.

- Feeling frustrated and disappointed during the early learning stages of dancing may result from your taking it too seriously. You may feel awkward while learning new steps because you have not yet experienced the feeling of mastering them. It is natural to make mistakes in the beginning. Later, with experience and confidence, you will execute complicated steps as well as experienced dancers do. A sense of humor while learning how to dance will help you relax and keep you interested and motivated. In other words, appreciate the bud as well as the rose!

Great inspiration comes through peace of mind.
***

*The deeper your awareness of who you are,
the more you can experience yourself.*
***

*The more you fear someone or something,
the more you will experience it.*
***

Be positive, and positive things will follow.
***

Do not let your mind control your life.
***

10

Chapter 10 Sources of Inspiration

Famous Dancers

There are many wonderful dancers who should always inspire you. Their passion for dancing is evident in their work: Gene Kelly, Fred Astaire, Ginger Rogers, Mikhail Barysknikov, Gregory Hines, and countless ballroom dance champions will be remembered for their romantic, poetic, and natural dance styles. While many dancers may not reach their same level of technical perfection, we can all aspire to achieve the enjoyment they exhibited. These dancers loved to improvise routines with their partners. Beauty is what they brought, and still bring, to dancing. They were passionate, romantic, and gentle, engaging the forces of nature and expressing their feelings through their dancing. They understood themselves, their music, their dancing, and their partners. They blended their movements into the rhythm and melody. These romantic and feeling dancers were themselves, and this confidence brought them popularity and fame. They were poetic through their facial expressions and their hand and body movements, inspired by the music and their partners. You too can learn to be in touch with all the elements of dance.

Quotations from Students

Each of the following paragraphs is the statement of a different student, explaining how dancing has helped that person to develop self-confidence:

"I started out dancing stiffly when I was a kid. In the 6th grade I loved my one year at dancing school, but at 12 I was naturally stiff because I was scared. Then we moved and no one in my new environment did the fox-trot or the Viennese waltz. Rock music left me cold. When I had to dance in high school at the junior and senior proms, and a few times later in life, I was terrified and you guessed it—still stiff.

"When I separated from my husband years later, I tried dance classes again. My good fortune was to find instructors who taught me usable steps. And then ultimately, a Latin dance instructor taught me to enjoy movement first and learn style later. During my first lesson with him, he had me waltz for five minutes with my eyes closed. Even I could feel the difference, the natural lilt to the beat. I relaxed. This instructor's approach allowed me to find myself as a dancer.

*

"I used to feel very uncomfortable with people watching me during my private lesson, because I was afraid to make mistakes in front of them. But after two years of taking private lessons, I do not feel shy any more. Instead, I enjoy showing off the little I know. I have also been teaching dancing to a couple of friends, and doing dance demonstrations with my partner. Let me tell you, it feels good!"

*

"A dancing figure is a very powerful figure. It is direct and forceful. It comes from the side of dreams and desires, the underside and inside of our most primitive and real selves. It is sensual and sexual and romantic and yearning. Our masks are exposed. Many people for this reason won't dance or, if they do, they dance "steps," like being a tree on a floating island. Dance may be taught this way as a gesture towards invulnerability since people on the dance floor want to feel safe, but it falls short of what it can be. My first lessons were like that. Then I came to a new instructor. He watched me with thoughtful intuition. He saw that I needed to learn to use my upper half with the same freedom as my lower half. I had grown up respecting logic and words above everything and my body was structured to this reality, so that the upper body was dedicated to control. The instructor pushed my tense shoulders down and used his own arms as models until I learned to move my arms unconsciously in space. It was intimidating and risky, but it paid off in the freedom I gained."

*

PART IV
COMPETITION—IS IT FOR YOU?

If you take things less personally, you will become healthier.
***

Life will treat you the way you treat yourself and others.
***

Competition leads to superiority and inferiority.
***

You never know your own talent until opportunities challenge you.
***

All superstitions are illusions.
***

All spirits are one and equal.
***

11

Chapter 11 Thinking It Over

Competitions are glamorous to watch and can encourage you to learn to dance and develop self-confidence. In addition it can be very rewarding to experience performing and showing your talent in front of an audience. However, you should consider the pluses and minuses of competing, whether you are an amateur or professional.

Advantages and Disadvantages

"Dance competition is required. It is the survival of the fittest and winning is the highest good."

This perception will produce losers, feelings of superiority, inferiority, and creates spiritual and emotional discomfort. It can also create expectations by the audience of their favorite couples rather than just enjoying everyone dancing their hearts out.

Dance competitions can be an outlet for performing and developing your self-confidence, for socializing and making friends in different places of the world, and for getting the experience of dancing in foreign countries. Competing can boost your popularly with members of both sexes who may like your dance style or personality as a professional dancer. Participating in competitions, and winning a few, will enhance your resume.

Competitors' average expense:

- Solo exhibition or Theater Arts, $50.
- International or American Style 5 or 10 dances, $200 to $400.
- Professional Rising Star, $125 to $400. Pro-Am, $100 to $300.
- Top teachers prices, $400 to $2,500.
- Scholarship prices, $100 to $500.
- Adult or Junior Formation Exhibition, $20 to $60.
- 2 or 3 days hotel accommodations and meals for two, $300 to $400.
- Dance costumes, $250 to $3000.
- Two or three pairs of dance shoes, $100 to $150 a pair.
- Amateur lessons a week, $210 to 350.
- Videos of your dance competition, $20 to $30.
- Transportation, $50 to $100.
- Travel, $200 and $400, or overseas Package per person, $1,300 to $2,400.
- Late fees, $25 to $35.
  Be aware of the following:
- Colorful dance outfits such as hot pink, turquoise, orange, red, and yellow can cheer up both you and your audience and help you look and feel glamorous. Dance outfits should match your personality and body language. For example, if you are a happy and assertive dancer, wear vivid colors; if you are conservative, wear black, blue or brown.
- Be outrageous and show some of your best steps at the beginning of your routine to spark your audience's interest.

- Silky shirts, blouses, pants or dresses can make you feel sensual while dancing or performing with others.
- Do not wear doubled-hemmed pants because your partner's heels may get caught in the cuff.
- Having the need to put on a happy face on the floor during a competition when you are feeling unhappy may not help you. You are always projecting your emotions to your partner and the audience whether you are feeling happy or unhappy. Deciding to be happy will lead you to being happy, or focus on a happy thought that will give you a genuine lift in soul that will carry though the dance routine.
- If you cannot afford it, competition can be a burden.
- It can be very stressful for professionals who are doing Pro-Am routines to do more than 10 entries.
- It is stressful if you must starve yourself to death to fit into your dance outfits.
- Traveling can be stressful.
- You may begin feeling insecure, jealous, anxious or overconfident before and during a competition.
- Your anticipation or judgmental attitude can keep you from enjoying yourself.

Preparation

This section contains tips for choosing an event where you might want to compete, getting your routine ready, and choosing appropriate apparel.

Choosing a Competition Environment

Amateur competitions are usually held in the mornings, afternoons, or weekends, rather than at night, which is the time reserved for professional competitors. Tickets should cost $10 or be free, to encourage more spectators to come to support amateur competitors. It can be difficult for your audience to attend an amateur competition that takes place during early morning hours on weekdays. Your fans and friends may find it difficult to come and watch you dance at those times, and it will be difficult for you to dance and become inspired when hardly anyone is watching you.

Amateur competitions at universities are often the most enjoyable to watch, because they are not as restrictive as professional competitions. Also, the university dance competition environment is more relaxed:

- Dancers are allowed to have different partners for different dances in the same competition. Also, the partner can be of the same sex—two women or two men can dance together.
- Most of the competitors in the University competitions are young and ambitious dancers. They are not modest; they are daring and ready to enjoy themselves and show their dance skills to the audience and to their partners.
- There is less tension, less preferential treatment, and the judges are generally friendly.
- The audience encourages and supports all the competitors.

Note: These competitions and the associated dance classes can be a very inexpensive opportunity for children and adolescents to learn to ballroom dance.

For amateur competitions, dance organizations should encourage DJs to play the music originally associated with a dance. For example, for a Latin dance competition, a DJ should play happy and romantic Latin songs or instrumental music. For modern dances such as Foxtrot or Quickstep, the DJ should play jazz music like Frank Sinatra or George Benson. When competitors are dancing a Samba, the DJ should be playing exotic Brazilian music in order for the audience to understand the cultural background of the dance and the music.

Be aware that some instructors may take you into competitions while you are still looking immature and awkward as a dancer. If your instructor does this, he/she is not taking the responsibility nor making the effort to train you properly to look your best on the dance floor. Perhaps your instructor is working with too many other students to have the time to choreograph a good routine for your level of competition. Some studios urge their students to compete for financial gain for their businesses without considering whether or not the student is really ready.

Preparing Emotionally

Many new dancers are not emotionally ready to confront the stress, meet with the expectations of judges and the audience, or meet their own expectations and possible disappointments in today's professional dance competitions. For instance, after receiving fourth or fifth place in a competition, dancers may lose their temper, leaving the competition because their expectations are shattered. Going to competitions to have fun, show your talent, and sell your business can be a lot more therapeutic and beneficial than winning a trophy.

First, you need to prepare emotionally for the event. However, some coaches may not know how to teach you to deal with the emotional challenges of competition and the politics involved. Here are some suggestions:

- Keep in mind that you are always a winner, no matter what the results of the competition, because the experience makes you a more advanced dancer and a more effective performer. Professionals may promote business but you will gain experience during competitions even as an amateur. In dance competitions there is never failure, only gained experience.
- Accept other people's dance talents and remember that there is always room for everyone to win something.
- Do not enter too many competitions if you do not want to burn out; remember that you need only compete in a few dances and do them well.
- Become acquainted with other competitors before and after the competition to promote a healthier environment.
- If you are stressing yourself out, you may also be stressing the judges, other competitors, and your audience. Take a deep breath and get in touch with the power of the present moment with your partner.
- Practice yoga for stretching, aerobic exercises to tone up your muscles, jogging for endurance in your legs, and meditation to relax your mind. Twenty years ago professionals simply practiced with their partners and competed the following week. Today understanding the importance of mental conditioning, competitors get massages, exercise, a good diet, and daily workouts to get ready for competitions.
- Upper body workout: If you have the tendency to push yourself too much when working your upper body (your emotional state), you become emotionally tough on yourself and others. However, if you do not work your upper body, it may suggest that you are not emotionally or mentally strong enough. In other words, if you are not moderate in your exercise, you may have hard times

dealing with your emotions if there are conflicts with your partner or loved ones.

- Lower body workout: If you push yourself too hard when working your lower body (your sexual state), you will become tough and demanding sexually toward yourself and others. Conversely, if you do not work your lower body it indicates that you are physically or sexually submissive. In other words, you may have a hard time sexually saying no to your partner.

- Most men believe that their bodies are machines, therefore, they push themselves to unhealthy limits. They should be listening to the language of their bodies to avoid physical pain.

Planning Your Routine

In the last decade, dancers have became more creative during dance competitions. For example, partners are choreographing impressive introductions for dance routines, giving themselves a whole new way to express their personal touch.

Some couples learn to make a lot of unnecessary facial expressions because they have not yet gotten in touch with their passion for each other, their dancing or their music. You can learn to make natural facial expressions if the music or your partner triggers you to do so. This can be effective when both you and your partner find passion in dancing with each other.

Music

Playing up-to-date music for a competition can provide variety and surprise, rather than using old music that many competitors have been dancing to for years. It may even be more challenging for you if the music has two dances in one song. Therefore, you and your partner must be alert. For example, If you are dancing a Mambo and suddenly the song takes on a slow tempo becoming a Rumba, the audience can appreciate how you change gears from one dance to another. Judges can see that you are adapting to the music and that you can improvise your routine rather than do it mechanically.

Whether you are an amateur or professional, altering your routine to your music during competition can be a most fun and impressive feat, because you will show your true talent. In order to improvise successfully, you need to feel the music and create mutually understood signals that will let you lead or follow the steps. You will be natural, less mechanical, and look more familiar with your music. If you are only doing an exhibition, it can be even more entertaining for you because there is no pressure associated with your performance, and the soul and art of the dance can be maintained. Later you will be able to do this during a competition.

In addition, if you and your partner want to make your routine more passionate or dramatic, you can create a story of heroes and victims, or star-crossed lovers, etc. This can make your audience pay more attention to your dancing.

Deciding What To Wear

A clean-cut hair style is recommended for men who are doing smooth dances such as Waltz, Fox-trot, or Tango, because it fits the suave personality of the dance. However, long hair can be fun for some men in dances such as Cabaret, Latin, and Theater Arts because it can project a sexier look.

The color of your clothing gives off a particular kind of energy and affects or compliments your emotions, from a soothing blue to a lively and energetic red to an earthy brown. Wearing bright colors makes you lively, happy and optimistic, and expresses your freedom and your sense of humor. However, behind some colors there are certain personality traits:

- Red suggests vigor, fire, and sexual passion. Wearing red can attract attention. If you have a passive personality, red, like other bright colors, may help you feel more assertive, fun and loving.
- Black suggests the opposite of other colors. Over the years people have learned that black is bad, representing fear and evil (even though evil does not exist). Black clothing can make you look cool as a dancer if you are in good shape, or have darker skin and hair. If however, in wearing black you are trying to project a macho image to intimidate or impress others, it is usually because you are covering your gentle side. Men are generally afraid of expressing their emotions because society has taught them not to be vulnerable on or off the dance floor.
- Pink is calm and relaxed. If you are a hyperactive dancer, wearing pink can calm you down. Pink is a favorite color for many women at dance competitions because of its softness.
- Blue is a majestic and cool feeling color. Wearing this color may project a regal or serious image.
- Yellow indicates hope, humor, and creativity. If you have the tendency to wear this color it is because you are expressing passion, optimism and humor.
- Green represents healing. If you are feeling down, wearing green may help you ease some of your pain.
- White indicates purity, cleanliness and neutrality. White is the essence and the base of all colors. Seldom is white worn in dance competitions, however, because it gets dirty quickly.
- Purple portrays spirituality. This color is hardly worn in the dance environment or dance competitions because it is more subdued. However, wearing this color may bring you more in touch with yourself.

- Brown represents the earth, the unemotional aspect. Wearing brown indicates that you may be mentally and emotional unavailable towards yourself and others. If you are feeling unemotional or mentally rigid, trying to wear colorful clothing may bring out your passion and humor.

The Impact of Tension

Stress before competitions can make it difficult for you to relax. There are both psychological and emotional pressures that you and your partner must deal with and you may have difficulty agreeing on your dance routines, outfits, coaches, and the many restrictions at the competitions. By the time the competition starts, you may not feel one hundred percent ready, especially if you are inexperienced.

Some things to watch for:

- If you become tense, your reflexes will slow down.
- If you are too eager to perform, you may forget your routine or affect your partner's performance (if your partner is tense, it can affect your lead or follow). It may help to think of this as simply another practice.
- If you are jealous of other dancers, you may do things such as pushing them unintentionally or getting in their way (however, there is no such thing as doing things unintentionally, because your actions are an act of self-definition whether you are doing it consciously or unconsciously).
- Few competitors just like to enjoy dancing, most are more serious and tense during competition. If there is excessive tension, some dancers can become overly aggressive and may try to intimidate other inexperienced competitors.

- If you show strong facial expressions while dancing, thinking that it will make you look more aggressive or passionate, it may be because you have not yet found your true personality and passion. Perhaps you are trying to impress your audience or you are doing it because you have been told this will make you a more expressive dancer. This may take away from your natural way of expressing your feelings.

- If you are an emotional dancer who is competing under a full moon, do not be surprised if you experience some emotional turmoil, because a full moon does stir up repressed emotions, making you release anxiety and become impulsive or insecure about yourself or your dancing (the first five days before a full moon, the healing process starts, and you may experience releasing some emotional baggage). Wearing pink may help you to feel more relaxed.

Emotions are thoughts in motion and not all emotions are feelings, in fact some emotions masquerade as feelings making you do things that you merely think are right. Emotions repeat themselves in your mind while feelings, which are the language of the soul, come unexpectedly. Unfortunately, we have the tendency to make our personal and business decisions upon our past emotional experiences, rather than making them through your present feelings, which would be healthier.

Response from the Audience

If you are a very sensitive and intuitive dancer, you can perceive how receptive or closed your audience is while you are performing or competing. For example, the audience may not respond well to your dance routine because you may be from out of town, making you feel nervous and causing you to forget some steps. If the two of you are from out of town and doing a solo performance, and you sense something strange about your environment or yourself, it is probably because your audience is holding back its feelings for you and want its favorite couple to win. Group consciousness can be very powerful because it affects how you feel in that present moment. When you compete, you can only do your best and have a good time. Do not go to win, go to enjoy the experience and you will always be a winner. However, if you have danced with the same partner for many years, the reaction of the audience may not affect you. Couples who are intimately involved or married may have an advantage because of their comfort and trust in each other against outside pressure.

Being Yourself

More and more professional competitors are demonstrating a sense of humor in their routines to entertain both themselves and their audience. This should encourage you to naturally express your humor, be yourself, and rejuvenate your mind, body and especially your soul, because your soul is joy.

In addition, more parents are performing with their teenagers at dance competitions, because their sense of security and closeness with each other can lead them to be more themselves. When family members grow and dance together, they can experience a unique closeness and enjoy good dance memories.

What the Judges Look For

Judging is a difficult job because it requires experience, talent and an understanding of the connection of the soul, mind, body, and music. Judges have been competitive dancers themselves, and some still coach to keep their philosophies about dancing current. However, every judge is different and each likes different things in different dancers. The requirements for Smooth dances may be more restrictive than for Rhythm dances for instance. However, judges all have their own priorities when evaluating competitors for technique and style.

In today's competitions judges are looking for competitors with good artistic interpretation, technique, style, dance outfits, and connection with each other. Judges should encourage competitors to improvise their routines in order to enjoy the music the judges selected. Improvisation can demonstrate that competitors can express themselves spontaneously through music, soul, mind, and body. Relaxing and having a good time on the dance floor is also helpful.

Judges usually are comparing competitors in the following:

- Body language before and after the music starts.
- Technique.
- Style.
- Communication skills.
- Grooming and dance outfits.
- Effortless movements.
- First impression.
- Posture.
- The ability to create artistic movements or illusions.

PART V
BODY LANGUAGE ON THE DANCE FLOOR

*When you give to others, you are giving to
yourself, and when you give to yourself, give to
others because we are all one.*
***

An unhealthy mind leads to an unhealthy body.
***

A stride expresses many messages.
***

*If you believe that you are imperfect,
you will do imperfect things.*
***

*Do not give a second thought to the things
you do not like.*
***

12

Chapter 12 Behavior Toward a Partner

Behavior while Leading

The way you lead your partner indicates how you interact with her emotionally and physically, both on and off the dance floor. Leading is one of the most important aspects of dancing, because it shows how you are going to communicate with your partner. What a woman likes to feel in her partner's lead is the ability to make her execute her steps successfully so she can maneuver gracefully across the dance floor.

Complicated Lead

Executing a difficult lead or complicated steps without much warning to your partner while dancing may indicate that you can be a difficult person. You may have the tendency to change your lead at the last minute, not giving enough time to your partner to think or follow you. In your personal life you may tend to be emotionally and mentally inflexible. Simplicity leads to less work and questions. When you make things easier for your partner, the two of you can have an easy and fun time.

Perfectionist Leader

If you are a perfectionist, you may need to dance with those who are at your skill level in order to enjoy yourself. You may become irritated with beginners. However, if you become intimately involved with your partner, you may become temporarily more patient. Being a perfectionist is another sign of extremism, making it more difficult to be flexible with others on and off the dance floor.

Passive Lead

Having a passive lead indicates that you are holding back your passion, assertiveness and self-confidence. Giving upper body resistance through your arms or tilting towards your partner may help you lead your partner more efficiently. Assertiveness is also an important aspect in dancing. If you dance with others who are mentally and physically strong, you need to have a strong and flexible lead. If your partner gives you strong upper body resistance, this will force you to lead more appropriately.

Passive dancers often attract partners with strong personalities, because it is an opportunity for them to develop what they have repressed or held back. By the same token, strong women may also attract men with passive personalities who lead slowly, because they need to learn to relax. If both you and your partner are passive dancers, your dancing may become boring to you because neither of you will create the fire or passion to enjoy it Active exercises or fast dances can help you improve your upper body resistance to become more confident.

Smooth and Flexible Lead

A consistent smooth and flexible lead demonstrates that you are a warm, tender, sensitive, compassionate, and flexible person. These traits are indicative of self-control, kindness, perception, and patience on and off the dance floor. You can make anyone feel comfortable because you are connecting to your partner and finding her rhythm. You can easily adjust your lead to different partners so they can follow you. You can be a very romantic dancer by expressing your feelings through actions and gestures on the dance floor.

Over-Enthusiastic Lead

If you are an over-enthusiastic leader who does not pay enough attention to your partner, you may be too involved with your feelings or emotions for your partner to follow you. You may need to relax and slow down in order to lead your partner properly. Slow dances such as the Waltz, Rumba, and Fox-trot can help you to control yourself and your dance movements.

Rough Lead

A rough lead may suggest that you are emotionally and physically inflexible to yourself and others because of your anger. You have the tendency to be controlling toward your partner or loved one because you may be afraid of losing her. When you first meet a new partner, you are more flexible, but after a while you begin to show your true colors. You may tend to blame others when things go wrong because you do not like to admit your mistakes. Releasing your anger through Reiki treatments or spiritual healing can be the fastest way to achieve a more flexible personality in your lead.

Hesitant lead

Having the tendency to hesitate while leading your partner may suggest that you keep changing your mind about your steps or are feeling anxious. You may be having difficulties making or improvising your decisions unless you have a plan. In dancing, learning routines may help you became less anxious and hesitant. The more you practice your lead with different partners, the more you can learn to adapt, and the more flexible you become on and off the dance floor.

Leading Two Partners

The tendency to lead and dance with two partners at the same time may indicate that you are projecting a playboy image or like the challenge of dancing with two different women. You may have the ability to emotionally and physically handle two different partners at the same time on and off the dance floor. You have great muscle coordination in both hands, which enhances your ability to dance with two partners, especially if there are more women than men in a group class.

Exaggerating your Steps

The tendency to exaggerate your steps while dancing indicates that you are trying too hard to prove yourself to others. You may be an inexperienced dancer who is working hard to look good. However, more experience may lead you to look more relaxed. It takes effort to make dancing look effortless.

Behavior while Following

The way you follow your partner's lead is often the same as the way you respond emotionally and physically in life. When you take an active role in following your partner, you are also learning to communicate and develop your social skills. Eye contact is required to follow your partner more appropriately. What a man likes to feel in his partner's following is her ability to give him her undivided attention without anticipating his next move.

Passive Following

If you provide little physical resistance to your leader it is because you may be showing a passive personality or holding back your passion for dancing. You may be having a hard time being assertive with your partner on and off the dance floor. Active physical exercises can help you develop physical and mental strength and improve your communication skills on the dance floor.

Not Following

Resisting your partner's lead often shows an inflexible personality on your part. If your leader is trying to accommodate you and you still are not responding, it is because the two of you may have very different chemistry. Resisting your partner's lead may also indicate that you are bossy, aggressive, and not used to taking orders from others on or off the dance floor.

Good Following

Good following is an indication that you are an easygoing, intuitive, warm, and flexible partner to different dancers. You are very aware of your surroundings on and off the dance floor and have a personality which adapts to different dances.

Pulling Your Partner

The tendency to pull your partner toward you while dancing may indicate that you are craving love and affection from others or needing companionship. You may be having difficulty finding a partner when you are going through self-introspection. However, this is another sign that you need to spend time with yourself so you can take care of yourself.

Pushing Away

If you have a tendency to push your partner away while dancing, it maybe because you are emotionally and physically protecting yourself due to unsuccessful past relationships, or you may be unconsciously perceiving negative vibes from your partner. However, healing your past unresolved relationships with others may help you become healthier and enjoy your dancing more.

Other Responses to Partner

Looking Behind

If you often look behind while dancing with your partner it is because you do not trust yourself or others. You want to make sure that your partner does not run into others or objects that may hurt you. However, improving your relationship with yourself in order to trust yourself more may help you to improve your relationship with your partner. Closing your eyes can be excellent practice while dancing with your partners, because it helps you to relax and trust them more. Sometimes you need to know your partners in order to trust them so you can feel secure.

Losing your Balance

The tendency to lose your balance while dancing may demonstrate that you may have feet problems, are putting too much weight on one foot, are experiencing dizziness, vision problems, or ear problems. Being too much in your head or mind also causes your body to elevate through your toes, making you less stable. Closing your eyes can help you think less, become less distracted and more grounded, which eventually can improve your balance. In addition, dancing with your feet flat on the ground may also help you to develop stability.

Level of Control

The ability to control your movements while dancing may suggest that you are practical and not too emotional. Conversely, too much control of your body movements while dancing can keep you from fully expressing yourself to the music, whether you are an experienced or inexperienced dancer.

Dancing in the Corner

The tendency to put your partner in a corner of the dance floor while following or leading may indicate that you are showing your aggressive and subduing personality. However, avoiding the corner by your partner may suggest that he/she is feeling uncomfortable, claustrophobic, trapped, or afraid of being physically and emotionally subdued. Sometimes dancing in corners is less difficult than dancing in the middle of a crowded floor because there is more space.

Dancing Alone

Dancing alone can be a sign of independence, lack of inhibition, or loneliness. Dancing on your own in a crowded room can make you more self-centered or selfish, which makes it harder to share and spend time with others. Remember that unity of two or more people brings inner strength, compassion and confidence.

Not Facing your Partner

If you have a hard time facing your partner while dancing or interacting, it suggests that you are protecting yourself from being emotionally or physically hurt. You may be having a hard time confronting your partner or others because you are verbally repressing your emotions.

Getting Physical

Getting physical while dancing with your partner demonstrates that you are sexually expressive on and off the dance floor. Your sexual thoughts and desires reflect in your dancing and cause you to move suggestively without necessarily intending to lead on others of the opposite sex. You may also enjoy dancing closely with different partners.

Macho Style

If you act "macho", it is because you are angry and have a confrontational attitude toward others. You have repressed your love, which makes you a controller, possessive, and obsessive toward your partner. You are afraid to show your gentle side, which you consider a weakness. In dancing, this macho image can only make you look tough and angry.

Reacting Negatively

Reacting negatively on and off the dance floor suggests that you have repressed your anger from past unhealthy and unresolved relationships. If someone steps on your foot or bumps into you, you may react negatively. You have the tendency to anticipate your pain before the impact. For instance, if your partner has the tendency to be late in getting ready to go out dancing, knowing that you like to leave on time, it is because she/he is unconsciously or consciously making you wait on purpose. You are in turn reacting to her/his actions and intentions. If your partner says things to you that bother you, or wants to get you angry, then you are reacting to her/his anger and behavior.

Feeling Intimidated?

If you are feeling intimidated practicing your dancing at some clubs, dance studios or restaurants for the first time, it may be because some of the people in this dance environment are projecting a judgmental, competitive, and selfish attitude towards you. Although this rarely happens, when they see that you are a new and good dancer, especially if you are an attractive and sexy dancer, they are unconsciously or consciously trying to protect their partners from you. This group of people is feeling threatened by you.

Becoming Subdued

If you unconsciously become subdued by your partner while dancing for no apparent reason, it may be that you are overwhelmed by her/his strong personality and chemistry. Your partner may be emotionally and mentally stronger than you and this is affecting your dancing by your being consciously more careful with her/him. Perhaps, this is also an indication that you are attracting the parenting type of partner.

A story of becoming subdued or tamed:

Bill is a dancer who usually likes to be in charge on the dance floor. He is very assertive and has a very particular dance style. However, sometimes he finds a partner with whom he becomes a pussycat. He appears to no longer be in control. Suddenly he becomes very careful and gentle and even wonders what is going on. He cannot explain why this is happening, but he feels good to have found someone who can control him (a mothering type). Later, they start dating and he finds out that he likes strong women.

Quietness

If you are usually quiet on and off the dance floor it may indicate that you like to communicate one-on-one with people. You are more effective dancing just with one partner most of the time. You can be mentally and emotionally sensitive or receptive if something does not work out with your partner (do not confuse sensitive with fragile. If you are emotionally fragile, you may tend to blame and hurt yourself. If you are emotionally sensitive, you are being more understanding of yourself and others and can let go of others when you need to).

Similar Dance Style

If you and your partner have similar dance movements, body language, or dance styles, it suggests that the two of you have similar thought patterns (like attracts like). Generally, if you and your partner have been dancing together for a long time, the two of you become receptive to each other's body language and personality. This can be an advantage in competitions because you communicate more intuitively with each other or guess each other's body language or steps. Verbal communication may not be needed.

The way you lead or follow is an expression of your personality.

***

The way you see the world is the way the world sees you.

***

A flexible personality is the key to a good lead or follow.

***

If you think you are too tough, you cannot be too gentle.

***

A partner who is gentle has a warm heart.

***

13

Chapter 13 Physique

This chapter is written as if you were looking in the mirror and analyzing your own physique. You may find that at certain times in your life, this is what interests you the most. At other times, you will find that you are more concerned with understanding the people around you. This chapter can also help you in that regard. Topics begin with general appearance, and then, beginning with the head, progress down to the toes.

It is important to understand that all mental, physical and spiritual problems begin in your mind, how you perceive your inner and outer world. However, by changing your thoughts and perceptions about life or yourself, you can heal your mental, physical and spiritual state.

General Appearance

General features of the body include height and weight as well as the amount of hair and the quality and temperature of the body.

Height

You may assume that people who are tall and physically strong are also both psychologically and emotionally stronger than those who are small or short, because society has taught you that big and physically strong are stronger and healthier than short and small. It is more important how strong you feel within yourself.

- If you feel taller than your actual height, it may suggest self-confidence, courage, and optimism about life. However, this may also be a sign of a strong ego.
- If you feel shorter than your actual height, it may indicate a lack of self-confidence and pessimism in your personality.
- If you are tall and overconfident, you may like to control your partner and become possessive. In dancing, by shortening your steps you can help your partner feel comfortable if she/he is shorter than you.
- If you are tall and lack self-confidence, you may attract a short and confident partner. In dancing this may help you feel more confident about yourself.
- If you are reluctant to dance with short partners, this may suggest that you are underestimating them or have a strong ego.
- If you find it difficult to ask tall partners to dance, you may be experiencing low-self-esteem.
- If you are short and like to dance with tall partners, this suggests that you have self-confidence or may be seeking emotional and physical protection.
- If you are tall and consciously or unconsciously shorten yourself while dancing with short partners, this may suggest that you are being considerate because you are trying to make her/him emotionally and physically comfortable. Do not forget to hold your partner's hand at your partner's chin level to make her/him feel and look comfortable while dancing in a close position.

Weight

As I mentioned before, all mental, and physical problems begin in your mind, because the way you perceive life is the way you are going to experience it.

Obesity

In this world of relativity you will experience its opposites, such as right and left, cold and hot, up and down, tall and short or fat and thin. Therefore, there is nothing wrong with being fat or thin, but healthy. However, if you are obese and unhealthy, it may be a reflection of holding back your personal desires. You have become lazy and have repressed what you want to do in life. Often, obesity can lead you into health problems or make you lose the desire for life. Therefore, too many distractions such as watching television, reading the newspaper or doing other things while eating, can affect your digestive system by causing you to retain more fat and water in your body. You are looking for emotional and physical attention, and becoming too involved with the outside world to avoid self-improvement. Verbally repressing your emotions and desires can also affect your thyroid, which in turn can affect your weight. Being obese or overweight can affect your dancing. Wear dark or slimming clothes to make you look slimmer.

Unfortunately, society perceives obesity as bad, and this perception discourages you from improving yourself and becoming healthier by doing and practicing the things you want to do in life. Caring too much about what other people think of you can contribute to your obesity.

Food intake may not always be the only reason you are overweight. Often you may lose weight but regain it later, because you have not yet released your repressed emotions and desires that caused you to gain weight in the first place. You need to change your perception about yourself, such as living up to your dreams and desires. Unconventional medicine such as Reiki treatments or other types of spiritual healing can help you release your repressed emotions and lose weight.

Many of you treat your bodies horribly because society makes you think that your body is a machine. Forced to push yourself to your limits, you later become mentally and physically burned-out and ill. Treating yourself more gently mentally and physically can help you regain some of your health so you can enjoy life. However, starving yourself to death because you want to look good, fit into your dance outfits to please your dance schools can lead you into anorexia. There are, for example, ballet schools that neglect students if they become too big or too tall. This is the most outrageous way to treat young students, encouraging them to look anorexic in order to fit a particular image. You may have everything, but without health you cannot enjoy anything.

Skin

The texture and temperature of your skin or body can be an indicator of your personality.

- Cold skin may indicate that you are physically, mentally, and emotionally hard on yourself and others. You may tend to be rigid with your ideas about life. In addition, if your back is cold, it may suggest that you are doing too much or taking on too many responsibilities for others. This may also lead to circulatory problems.
- Rough skin may suggest that you are physically and mentally a hard worker. However, you may be physically and emotionally rough with your partners on and off the dance floor.
- Soft skin may indicate that you are a sensitive or intuitive dancer, easygoing on and off the dance floor.

- Warm skin may indicate that you are easygoing and compassionate towards yourself and others.

Body Hair

The amount of hair on your body can indicate certain characteristics in your personality. This is especially true when the pattern of body hair is not the usual one for a person's sex.

- If you are a man and have very little hair on your body such as your arms, legs, chest or upper-lip, it may suggest your female characteristics or right-brain dominance. You can easily understand and get along with women.
- If you are a woman who has considerable hair on your arms, legs, and upper-lip as well as some masculine looks or personality, it may suggest that you have some male traits or left-brain characteristics (tomboy). You feel more comfortable being with men than women.
- A hairy upper body suggests that you may be emotionally and mentally hard on yourself and others. You may have the tendency to behave or express more your left-brain characteristics.
- A hairy lower body indicates that you may be physically and sexually hard on yourself and others. You may have the tendency to behave or express more your left-brain characteristics. In general, having more body hair provides you with a mental as well as physical shield from the outside elements.

Scalp and Brow Area

Much can be noted by observing the scalp and brow.

Gray Hair

Having premature gray hair may indicate excessive think-ing or taking too many responsibilities on yourself. You may spend too much time thinking about and focusing on your personal and work environment.

Baldness

Baldness may indicate that you are the controlling type of individual. You have repressed your love towards yourself and others and have become possessive. In addition, your exces-sive thinking can cause you so much mental tension that over the years, you may lose your hair.

Redness on the Scalp

Redness on the scalp is also a sign of excessive thinking, frustration, or stress because the concentration of thoughts (energy) around the brain becomes trapped for long periods of time. You are retaining a lot of heat or repressed anger around your head; this may be the reason why you may be having headaches. Listening to your feelings rather than your exces-sive thinking is the natural way of finding solutions to your conflicts.

Swollen Temples

Swollen temples may indicate that you have the tendency to lose your temper. In other words, you may have repressed your anger and have become mentally and emotionally rigid by not accepting other people's ideas. In such cases, stress, another person, or anything else getting in your way causes your temples to swell and you to lose your temper. This trait may be accompanied by redness in your face. Some dance coaches and many basketball coaches have swollen temples because they tend to react too much to the outside world. Patience hardly exists for them. Eventually this can lead to heart problems.

If your teacher has this physical trait, he/she may become frustrated and lose his/her temper if you are taking too long to learn your steps. You may need an instructor who is more patient while you are learning to dance.

Bumpy Forehead

A bumpy or puffy forehead indicates that you are very hard on yourself and others. Imagine someone with this physical trait hitting his/her forehead against the wall in desperate moments of frustration. Frustration is caused by your closed-minded personality and your impatience. Taking things less seriously can help you to ease your mind.

Playful Eyebrows

Eyebrows protect your eyes from sweat or outside elements, but the thickness of your eyebrows and the way you move them can express certain personality traits on and off the dance floor: If you have the tendency to raise and lower your eyebrows in a flirtatious way, it indicates that you are a physical, sexual, optimistic, and playful individual.

Furrows Between the Eyebrows

Furrows are not just features that make you look different, but they also reveal something about you. For example, a crease between your eyebrows shows that you have constantly and deeply questioned yourself about something from your inner or outside world. You may tend to push yourself mentally in looking for answers, but without much success. Patience and knowing may be the key to your quest.

One Eyebrow Higher

If your right eyebrow is higher than your left one, it is an expression of left-brain dominance. The excessive use of the right eyebrow can eventually cause it to stay a little higher than the other one. When you are consciously controlling any part of the right side of your body, you are using your left brain. If your left eyebrow is higher than your right one, you are demonstrating some of your right-brain characteristics.

Scanty Eyebrows

Scanty eyebrows indicate that you may be having a hard time expressing your ideas or protecting yourself emotionally and physically from others. It is hard to say "No" to others. Because there is little hair on your eyebrows, there is also little protection for your eyes. You may also allow people or things get in your way from achieving your personal goals.

High-Set Eyebrows

High-set eyebrows indicate that you may be emotionally and physically defensive towards others. You have the tendency to react negatively toward outside elements or people. You may have repressed negative emotions that have not yet been released or resolved. These high-set eyebrows may contribute to a tense look on and off the dance floor. If you have an instructor with this feature, you may have a hard time interacting with him/her because he/she may be impatient if you keep making mistakes while learning to dance. Patience and understanding are good traits for teaching. However, if you have high-set eyebrows and have a happy facial expression, it usually indicates a curious, optimistic, and outgoing dancer.

Bushy Eyebrows

Bushy eyebrows may indicate that you are a single-minded person who does not allow anyone or anything to get in your way. You may have strong will power, and can be very determined when you decide what you want out of life or dancing. You may also have a tendency to protect yourself from the outside world, and may not be open to new dance styles or techniques when it comes to improvisation.

V-Shaped Eyebrows

Having V-shaped eyebrows indicates that you may have a tough personality. You can be tense, frustrated, and tend to be physically and emotionally hard on yourself and others. This attitude can create health problems in the long term. In dancing, you may give the impression that you are feeling angry or tough. However, if you can become more gentle on yourself, you may also become more gentle with others on and off the dance floor (if you treat others badly, others are going to treat you the same way—remember that we are all one).

Eyes

Eyes are the windows of your soul through which others can see your true nature and tell how you feel about yourself and others. However, the way you perceive or see life through your eyes can be very deceiving, because you bring your own interpretations to what you see into your mind. Eye contact with your partner while dancing can help you follow or lead more effectively. However, if you are not giving eye contact while dancing, it can make it harder to focus or anticipate what your partner is going to do.

Size of Eyes

Big eyes suggests that you may be paying too much attention to the outside world. In other words, you may worry what others think about you. You may also need recognition from others in order to feel good about yourself. However, if you have small eyes, it may indicate that you are more involved with your own world. You are an idealistic and creative dancer who does not worry what others think of you.

Fiery Eyes

Fiery eyes may indicate that you are passionate, possessive, domineering, and confident. You are a competitive dancer and very protective of your loved ones and friends. However, if you are possessive and dominant towards your loved ones it is because you are repressing your love, or not accepting others for who they are.

Bulging Eyes

Bulging eyes suggest that you can be impulsive and emotionally fragile. In other words, you can be easily hurt. You tend to lose your temper if something goes wrong in your personal life with your loved ones. You make decisions based on your needs, emotions or past experiences. Insecurity is your great obstacle. Emotions are connected to your physical body and it can be hard to control your movements while dancing. You may be having a difficult time letting go of your partner or loved ones because you become easily attached. However, you can be compassionate, and like to help others in time of need. If you learn to control your dance movements, you may be able to control your emotions on and off the dance floor. Dancing with your eyes closed can be an excellent exercise to develop trust towards yourself and others. You can eventually become an excellent and expressive dancer.

Watery or shiny eyes may indicate that you are an emotional, sensitive, and less impulsive person. You are warm and compassionate. Staying in good shape mentally and physically through dancing can help you develop confidence.

Deep-set Eyes

Deep-set eyes may indicate that you are mentally grounded, practical, and not too emotional. You tend to be ruled more by your head than your feelings. Becoming more in touch with your feelings can help you balance the mind. In dancing, you may look too cool or mechanical if you do not show your feelings or emotions. If you are taking lessons from someone with deep-set eyes, you may have an easy time learning because they can be practical and easygoing individuals.

Squinting

If you tend to squint, it is probably because you have been forcing your eyes to read without reading glasses, and therefore forced your eyes to shrink in order to focus. In addition, chronic sinus problems may also contribute to squinting.

Farsightedness

Farsightedness is an indication that you have been avoiding interaction with others. You may be emotionally and physically detached from others or the outside world, because you like being in your own world. You are self-centered, which allows you to take care of and love yourself first before loving and taking care of others. Writing in big letters usually indicates an individual who is farsighted. You are introverted and may enjoy knowing about spirituality. Most older people become farsighted because they need to be more in touch with themselves.

In such cases the cornea is also slightly flat or dented, giving the impression that your cornea is pulling energy from the outside. If you do not wear reading glasses, you have to bring objects closer to your eyes in order to see them more clearly. Therefore, you may not be too meticulous on and off the dance floor, because you cannot see or notice small things. Being a perfectionist may not be your thing. However, becoming more emotionally and intellectually involved with others can bring you more harmony. If your instructor is farsighted, he/she may unconsciously neglect little details about your dancing.

Nearsightedness

Nearsightedness may suggest that you are neglecting your inner world or spending too much time living your life for others. You may tend to become involved in other people's business or help everyone but yourself. If you are nearsighted, you can be a great humanitarian. You tend to write small, because you do not want to be too obvious to others. You may be secretive when sharing personal things with others.

Your cornea is shaped like a football, giving the impression of pushing something out. You need to wear glasses in order to see the world farther away from you. You are a perfectionist because you see things very closely. However, if you become more in touch with your own inner world, it can help you balance your state of mind. With today's medical technology, both farsightedness and nearsightedness may be corrected by laser eye surgery.

One Eye Higher

If your left eye is higher than your right one, it is because you are showing your right brain characteristics. On the contrary, if your right eye is higher than your left one, you may be expressing your left-brain dominance.

Covering Eyes with Hair

Covering your eyes with your hair suggests that you are repressing your identity or self-esteem. You are also allowing people or things get in your way. In dancing, it can be very hard to show your facial expressions if your hair covers your eyes. You can see your audience, but you do not want your audience to see you. Pulling your hair back from your eyes and face can help you show more of yourself while taking dance lessons or competing, and eventually you will feel more comfortable with the outside world.

Covering your Eyes

Wearing sunglasses may help you protect your eyesight from strong sun rays, but how and where you wear them may say something about you.

If you have the tendency to wear sunglasses indoor and out suggests that you may be hiding some weak aspects of your personality that you do not want others to see. Perhaps you are trying to play and look cool. On the other hand, if you avoid wearing sunglasses, it is because you like to see people and things crystal clear.

Eyelashes

Society has taught you that long eyelashes are more beautiful than short ones. Eyelashes protect your eyes from dust and lint, but the length of your eyelashes can also express something about yourself:

Short eyelashes indicate that you may have a hard time protecting yourself from others or outside elements. You may not like to confront others because you are afraid of rejection or you may allow others or things get in your way. However, long eyelashes may indicate that you are overprotecting yourself from others. Long eyelashes do enhance facial expression and can make your eyes look bigger. Thus in dance competitions most women choose to wear fake eyelashes for extra drama.

Looking at the Audience

Looking at your audience while dancing or competing usually indicates that you are craving attention and recognition from others. You may have the need to prove yourself to the world. Self-appreciation may lead to wanting less recognition from others. However, if you are performing, you may like to look at your audience to invite them to participate in the entertainment.

Being Watched

If you do not like being watched by others while you are taking private lessons, it suggests that you have not yet developed self-esteem in your dancing or you do not want to make mistakes in front of others. You may tend to worry about what others think of you. Taking group lessons may help you become less shy about your dancing. Repetition of your dance steps or movements can help you build up your confidence.

Shape of Nose

The size and shape of your nose can tell you something about yourself. For example, a pointed, up-turned nose indicates that you are a thinker, impatient, a dreamer, or gullible. However, if you have your nose pointing downward (eagle nose), you are patient, self-centered, and compassionate.

A short nose indicates that you may be sociable, tactless, a loner, and hard on yourself and others. At times you can be honest and straight forward, regardless of how others feel emotionally. You usually communicate with others through actions rather than with words. Conversely, having a long nose indicates that you are patient, warm, creative, and sociable.

Dimples

Dimples can add charm to your physical character, but it can also tell you something about yourself. For instance, a dimple on your right cheek indicates that you are left brain dominant. A dimple on your left cheek suggests that you are right-brain dominant. Dimples on both cheeks indicate that you are both right and left-brain dominant.

High Cheekbones

High cheekbones may indicate a confrontational, or defensive personality. This may be another sign of repressed angry emotions. You like to take the law into your own hands. Dramatic Latin dances may fit your personality and looks.

Blushing

Blushing is a sign of embarrassment, a response to making mistakes or evidence that you are feeling angry or lying to someone. In addition, having a red face is an indication of impatience and a short tempered personality (you have retained repressed negative emotions around your head which later manifests itself on your face creating the redness). Alcohol can also make your face red because it triggers negative memories and repressed emotions. Exercises such as aerobics, running, playing racquetball or fast dances can help you release your stress and anger.

Ears

Your ears are the channels for receiving wisdom and advice, but how you receive or perceive the information can affect or trigger your emotions and perceptions about yourself and others. Therefore, you are responsible for the way you interpret instructions or information from your mind or feelings. If you interpret outside information through your mind, you may not go too far, because you may be creating yourself out of the experience of others. In other words, you have been told what to think, say, and do. However, if you listen to information through your own feelings, then you can make wiser choices, which can lead to peace of mind and happiness.

Size and Firmness of Ears

- Ears that are hard, small and close to your head indicate that you do not like to listen or take advice from others. You may be idealistic or rigid with your value system. It may take you a long time to grow up in life.
- Ears that are large, small, but soft may indicate that you are a great listener and very sensitive to music and sounds. You are also patient, intellectual, and receptive to inner wisdom.
- Ears that are protruding may indicate that you have the tendency to be very open to the outside world, and it can influence you in your decisions. If your left ear protrudes more than the right, it suggests that you are open to

other people's good and unconditional ideas. You can evolve much faster when you experience positive ideas from others.

- If you have your right ear protruding more than the left one, it indicates that you are open to conditional ideas from others. Therefore, if you are not careful who your friends are, you may absorb negative attitudes.
- If your left ear is higher than the right one, you are showing your right brain characteristics, because your left ear is closer to the brain.
- If your right ear is higher than the left one, it demonstrates your left brain dominance.

Hearing Difficulties

Hearing difficulties suggests that you may have closed yourself to new ideas and to the outside world. In addition, your rigid ideas can make it harder to understand other dancers with strong accents. Do not just listen with your ears, but listen with your soul so that you can *feel* what the others are saying. Accepting others for who they are can help you pay more attention and improve your hearing and feeling for what they are saying. Your hearing difficulties may also cause you to have a hard time understanding details about your dancing.

Mouth, Lips and Teeth

Your mouth, lips, and teeth can reveal some aspect of your personality:

Lines around Mouth

If your mouth points downward at the corners, it may indicate that you are a pessimist or a complainer. You have not yet let go of your repressed anger towards others. You may be hard on yourself and others and difficult to please. In dancing, this facial expression may give the impression that you are feeling sad or angry. However, if the corner of your mouth points up it suggests that you are optimistic and happy (people who complain too much usually attract or create problems so they can keep complaining, because what you are, you also project).

Protruding Mouth

Any physical exaggeration in your body may also show an extreme personality. A protruding mouth may indicate that you are verbally aggressive and defensive towards others. If you have problems with your teeth or gums, it is because you have repressed stress in your mouth by not expressing yourself verbally. In dancing, a protruding mouth may give the impression that you are complaining or being aggressive, but if you smile it may bring out your charm.

Difficulty Opening Mouth

If you have difficulty controlling the right side of your mouth, you may be verbally repressing your left brain characteristics. However, if you have difficulty opening the left side of your mouth, you may be holding back some of your right-brain aspects.

Size of Lips

• A thin upper lip indicates that you are holding back your emotions and feelings towards others. You may not be expressing how you feel about someone or something because you may think that it is a weakness to show your emotions.

- A thick upper lip indicates that you can freely express your emotions and feelings. You may be impulsive at times or make decisions when your emotions rather than listening to your feelings or your heart. The heart is the door to your soul and mind.
- A thin lower lip is a sign that you may be having difficulties expressing your sexuality or are being too sexually demanding toward your loved ones.
- A thick lower lip may indicate that you have a strong sex drive and are a giving individual.

Spaces Between the Teeth

Spaces between your teeth may indicate that you are verbally and emotionally expressive. You have the tendency to be direct and do not like to beat around the bush with others. On the other hand, if your teeth are so close to each other that you cannot even floss, it may indicate that you are mentally rigid and holding back your emotions towards others. You may have a hard time confronting others, because you are afraid of rejection.

Voice

The sound of your voice can be a very important personal characteristic, because it can reveal how you feel about yourself. There are several types of voices as follows:

Trembling Voice

A trembling voice may be an indication that you are feeling fearful, nervous, or lack self-confidence. In addition, a trembling voice can be triggered by someone who is trying to intimidate you. You may have experienced traumatic events in your early childhood that you have not yet let go. Having a trembling voice while teaching dancing may give the impression that you are inexperienced.

Loud Voice

Speaking loudly may indicate that you are feeling angry or are suffering from impaired hearing. If you cannot hear yourself too well, you will raise your voice to hear yourself loudly. Impaired hearing can be caused by blasting your ears with music from nightclubs or boom boxes, and strong noises from heavy machinery. In dancing, a loud voice can be an advantage while teaching, because you may not need a microphone.

Low-Pitched Voice

A low-pitched voice among teenagers may suggest maturity. However, if you are a woman, this may indicate that you are expressing your masculinity or your left-brain characteristics. However, if you speak very quietly, it may indicate that you are holding back your assertiveness or passion for someone or something.

High-Pitched Voice

If you are a man with a high-pitched or a young voice, you are showing a right-brain characteristic. This is another indication that you have a natural youthfulness. You also have a playful and easy-going personality.

Heavy Accent

If you have a heavy accent while communicating with others, you may be showing your strong value system. You may also be having a hard time adapting to a new environment due to this. You may have trouble getting others to understand you because of your heavy accent, especially if you are from another country. Being more receptive and open minded could help others to understand you more clearly. When others become emotionally and psychologically unavailable, they also become too rigid to listen to you.

Coarse Language

The tendency to use coarse language while interacting with others on and off the dance floor can be an expression of anger. In addition, using coarse language with your loved ones suggests that you harbor rage.

Breath

Fresh breath is very important when interacting closely with others while dancing or teaching. Bad breath on the other hand, can turn off your dance partner. However, brushing, flossing, and scraping your tongue after eating can help eliminate your bad breath. "Tic Tacs" or chewing gum may temporarily be a solution to mask bad breath while dancing in a close position. Eating fresh red pepper can also help eliminate bad breath.

The causes of bad breath may be the following:

- Cavities.
- Foods caught between your teeth.
- Stomach problems.

Neck

The neck holds and supports the head, and represents the stability of your perception and emotions. Therefore, the size of your neck reveals some aspects of your personality:

- A thick neck suggests that you may not be too emotional. You are practical and mentally strong, and you do not allow your emotions to control your decisions. An emotional partner can help bring out your natural emotions. A thick neck with protruding eyes may indicate that you are mentally and emotionally in conflict. However, because you cannot decide one way or the other, you may need to listen to your feelings in order to make constructive decisions.

- A thin neck is an indication that you are a thinker, a dreamer, impulsive, spiritual, and emotional. You have your head in the clouds, and give the impression that your head is delicate and fragile. You make decisions based upon your emotions or your heart.

- A short neck suggests that you are down to earth and practical about your ideas. You may be repressing your inner wisdom and spirituality. You are satisfied with the things you have, whether a little or a lot. If you have pain or discomfort in the back of your neck it is because you are repressing your personal desires or goals. You are not a risk taker (babies who hold and control their necks at a very early age or a few weeks after birth often will be emotionally and mentally strong and independent).

Prominent Adams Apple

Having a prominent Adam's apple may indicate that you do not easily admit your errors or mistakes to others. Furthermore, you may have difficulty revealing any emotional weakness to others, because you may think that it is not appropriate. This physical characteristic is usually seen more in men than women, because women are more open to their emotions and to admitting their mistakes and errors. In addition, having a double chin indicates that you may be verbally repressing your feelings to your loved ones.

Torso

This section includes the torso but not the limbs.

Upper Body

The upper body represents communication of the emotional and intellectual aspects, but how well this is expressed or repressed can affect the posture and the upper body.

If your upper body is proportionately larger than your lower body and you have some health problems, it may suggest that you are verbally repressing your emotions. Repressing your emotions will contribute to more weight gain on your upper body, by first affecting your digestive system and causing you to retain more water or fat. The more you repress your emotions, the bigger your upper body may become, and health problems will increase. In dancing, you may appear ungainly. Exercise such as fast dancing, running, and playing basketball may help you release your repressed emotions, but changing your perception about life would do more. Additional problems with your joints in your arms, hands, and shoulders indicate that you may need to be mentally and emotionally more flexible towards yourself and others.

Breasts or Chest

Again in the world of relativity you may be consciously or unconsciously experiencing its opposites, such as big and small, right and left, up and down, fat and thin, hot and cold. Breasts represent self-nurturing and the size of your breasts can reveal some traits about your personality:

- Small breasts indicate that you may be having a strong need to nurture others before yourself.

- Medium size breasts suggest that you are equally nurturing to yourself and others.
- Large breasts indicate that you may have a strong tendency to nurture yourself and others.

Whether you have small, medium or large size breasts and have the tendency to nurture others first, you may be taking the risk of having breast problems later because you are putting others before yourself. It is important that you become self-centered so you begin to take care of and love yourself first. Do not confuse self-centeredness with selfishness. When you are self-centered you like to give to yourself and share with others, but when you are selfish you like to give to yourself, but do not like to share with others. Men who love large breasts usually have a strong need to be physically and emotionally cared for. They have probably had many people taking care of them while growing up, especially women, and therefore are naturally attracted to large breasts. However, if you like small breasts, you may enjoy taking care of others.

Breast Cancer

Society is spending tremendous amounts of money and time searching for the causes of breast cancer. In addition, they are spending too much time on the symptoms of the problem rather than the cause of it.

It is important to understand that you are a soul (God) with a body and not a body with a soul. This can help you understand that your mind causes the problems that affect your body. However, if you believe that you are a body with a soul, you will try to cure the body or the symptoms before considering the importance of the mind or thoughts that cause your state of health.

Breast cancer indicates that for quite sometimes you have repressed your own self-nurturing whether you are a man or a woman. Lack of self-nurturing affects the energy field (aura) first around your breasts before creating the physical problem. To prevent breast cancer you need to learn to take care of yourself mentally, physically and emotionally before taking care of others. Physical, psychological or emotional trauma caused by others may have also contributed to breast problems. In addition, having health problems in your left breast may suggest that you are repressing your right brain characteristics. Having health problems in your right breast may indicate that you are holding back your left brain dominance (see page on brain dominance).

Breast Implants

Having breast implants suggests that you want to enhance your body image, have the need to be more attractive or desirable, or want to develop self-confidence. This has been a controversial issue mainly for health reasons. For instance, any physical alterations can create some health complications when your body rejects them if you do not change your perception about yourself. After having breast implants, you need to become more self-nurturing in order to help your implants remain healthy in your body. In addition, spiritual healing such as Reiki treatments or other types of spiritual healing will help you accelerate the natural healing process of your body before and after medical treatments.

Ribs and Waist

A wide ribcage (big waist) may indicate that you have great mental and physical endurance. You can carry more air in your lungs. In dancing, having a wide waist may give the impression of being overweight. Wearing clothing that is designed appropriately, such as shirts with side panels, can help your waist appear smaller.

ITI

Chest Out

If your chest naturally sticks out, it demonstrates that you are generally feeling confident. However, if you tend to force your chest out, it suggests that you are protecting yourself emotionally from others. You are creating an armor around your chest and not allowing others to get close to you. In the Armed Forces, you learn to stick your chest out, but this may not mean that you are naturally confident, because you simply learned to follow orders and respect your superiors (although superiority is an illusion, because we are all equal, but different).

A collapsed chest is caused by repressed negative emotions and unresolved past relationships with your loved ones. You have kept the pain and bitterness from past experiences without verbally expressing or revealing them to others, nor have you forgiven. You have been very secretive about this personal issue. This collapsed chest may also create a slight hunchback in the center of your back. However, verbally expressing these issues may help you release your repressed emotions. In dancing, a collapsed chest may give the impression that you are tired.

Lower Body

The lower body represents contact with the earth, physical endurance, sexuality, grounding, practicality, and independence. If your lower body is proportionately larger than your upper body, and you have some health problems in these areas, it suggests that you are repressing these elements of your personality. Additional problems with your knees and ankles indicate that you may need to be mentally and emotionally more flexible towards yourself and others.

Large Belly

A large belly may indicate that you have been repressing interaction with yourself and your loved one openly and unconditionally. Repressing your emotions, feelings or desires affects your physical body causing imbalances in your digestive system or thyroid, making your body retain more water and fat.

Since all mental and physical problems begin in your mind, you may need to change your perceptions or your thoughts about life, so you stop holding back your emotions, feelings or desires. Spiritual healing such as Reiki will help you release your repressed emotions and reduce the size of your belly.

Buttocks

Large buttocks indicate that you have a strong sex drive. Just as small or flat buttocks may indicate that you may be repressing your sexuality. If you tend to be demanding with your loved ones before having sex, you may also be taking a chance for others to put demands on you. This conditional attitude may lead to eventually losing your loved ones.

Pregnancy

Gentle dances such as the Waltz, Rumba, Foxtrot, as well as swimming can be healthy exercises during your pregnancy, because they can also relax your baby. Listening to rhythmic and happy music during pregnancy can help develop your baby's sense of rhythm. For example, by tapping your stomach with your hands to the tempo of your music during your pregnancy, your baby will develop a relationship with sounds.

Upper Limbs

The arms, and especially the hands, can provide a wealth of clues to personality.

Arms

Large and strong arms and hands may indicate that you enjoy strong physical labor. You are mentally and physically strong. However, small and gentle arms and hands may indicate that you are a practical and intellectual individual. Women who have large and strong arms may be showing some of their left-brain characteristics such as their masculinity and tomboyish personality. They enjoy socializing with male friends more than with women. However, if they are unhappy, becoming in touch with their right-brain characteristics may help them to balance their mental state. In dancing, women who have large and strong arms may lose some of their femininity on the dance floor. Long sleeves will cover your large and strong arms if you are uncomfortable showing them.

Men with skinny arms or legs may be expressing their feminine traits or their right-brain characteristics. This may also indicate that they can get along well with women, because women are naturally right brained and open to men who are also right-brain dominant. In dancing, men with skinny arms may look weak or feminine, but do not underestimate their strength.

Wrists

A thick wrist indicates that you are intellectual and analytical, and enjoy reading. You may also enjoy expressing your love through poetry. However, knowledge or intelligence (information) is only conceptual, and if you do not practice what you read or preach, you will never know truth or the experiential aspect of life. You are here in this life to experience what you already know in your spirit.

A thin wrist may suggest that you are more practical than emotional and enjoy expressing your love through action rather than through words. You may enjoy dancing, gardening, painting and massage.

A too flexible wrist while holding hands and dancing with a partner may suggest that you are mentally and emotionally somewhat submissive, or too flexible to the outside world. You may have a hard time standing up to others because of your insecurities (all insecurities are illusions, avoid them).

Wrists Elevated

Having your wrists elevated while you are lying down suggests that you have a defensive personality. You may have the tendency to negatively react towards others due to your repressed anger. It is important to remember that you are not your past, or your yesterdays, you can always change your present behavior to make your future healthier.

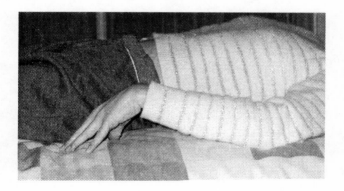

Wrist sticking up

JTI

Bending the Wrist

The tendency to bend your partner's wrist backwards while dancing may suggest that you are showing your domineering personality. You may have the tendency to control your loved ones because you have repressed your love (acceptance).

Bending her wrist backwards

Hands

Your hands are the tools and expressions of your soul, mind and body, but the shape and temperature of your hands can reveal some things about your personality:

Square Hands

Having square hands may indicate that you are prone to restrictions, rules and conditions. You see the world in

black or white. You can also be emotionally and psychologically hard on yourself and others.

Veined Hands

Veined hands suggest that you have a strong personality, both mentally and emotionally. You may be comfortable revealing your true colors to people. You can be a gentle
individual, but when others try to take advantage of you,
you can become tough and assertive.

Fingers

The shape of your fingers can give you clues to your
personality:

Space Between Fingers

Having spaces or windows between the fingers suggests
that you are generally an open minded person. However,
the bigger the spaces between your fingers, the more gullible you might be, especially to authority figures such as
dance teachers, priests, doctors, and lawyers, etc. You may
also have a hard time saving money for the future, because
you enjoy living in the moment. However, if you do not
have spaces between your fingers, you are a generally closed
or narrow-minded person. In other words, you may be going through hard times in life.

Spaces between your fingers on your right hand indicates that you are open minded to your left-brain aspects.
However, if you have spaces between your fingers on your
left hand, it may suggest that you are open minded to your
right-brain characteristics.

Having no spaces or windows between your fingers may
indicate that you are an idealistic or closed-minded indi-

vidual. You have a very strong value system and do not like to take advice from others. You may need to become open to new ideas if you are having a hard time in life. In life nothing remains the same way.

Short Fingers

Short fingers (smaller than your palms) may suggest that you have difficulty grasping or achieving great personal things in life. You may need to work harder in order to achieve your goals. You have to make opportunities to create more jobs. However, if you have long fingers, you have the capacity to grasp and achieve great personal things in life. You do not need to look for things you want, they will come to you.

Fingernails

Fingernails can be used as protection, tools or weapons. The shape, length, and strength of your nails can be a clue to some characteristics of your personality:

- Long and strong fingernails suggests health. They can be used as tools to scrape things or as weapons to defend yourself. Feeling your partner's nails while dancing may be a sign of her defensiveness.
- Soft and weak nails may suggest that you are having a hard time confronting others. This may also be a sign of calcium deficiency. Exercises, and a special diet may be needed to build mental and physical strength.
- Short, strong and clean nails may indicate that you are harmless, organized, or physically and emotionally strong. However, dirty nails may be a sign of neglecting yourself and others.

Interlocking Fingers

Interlocking your fingers with a partner while dancing may suggest that you are feeling secure and emotionally available.

Fingers Extended Downward

Having your fingers extended downwards with a tense look while walking, dancing or interacting with others indicates that you are angry and frustrated. You may be looking for a fight in order to release your repressed anger and frustrations. In dancing, extending your hands down may give the impression that you are feeling tense.

Fingers Extended Upward

Having your fingers extended upwards while holding hands with a partner in a close position when dancing may suggest that you do not want to become emotionally or physically attached or committed. You want to remain sexually and emotionally available to others. Your fingers may be barely touching your partner's right or left hand, avoiding connection.

Fingers extended upwards

Lower Limbs

No less than other parts of the physique, the legs and feet provide insights about yourself and others.

Legs

Having long legs may indicate that you have physical and sexual endurance, and the ability for great achievements in sports. You may be an outdoor type individual who enjoys different sports. You may not be too emotional in your love relationships. However, becoming in touch with your emotions and feelings can help you feel mentally and physically more balanced. In dancing, long and strong legs can be a visual asset. Conversely, having short legs may indicate that you have to make more effort to achieve your personal goals in sports, but intellectually you can have great achievements. You may be an intellectual individual who enjoys reading a lot, but if you put your intelligence or information into practice, you can efficiently experience what you already know.

Having a lot of heat in your lower legs may suggest that you are not exercising enough. In other words, the burning sensation or itching in your legs is an indication that you are retaining a lot of heat. You can release the heat by doing daily exercises such as walking, running, or fast dancing.

Bow-legs

Having bow-legs indicate that you may be sexually open-minded, and you may enjoy having more than one partner if you do not get enough from just one partner. In addition, having bow-legs and putting more weight on the outside of your feet may indicate that you enjoy making others sexually happy before yourself (it is also important to know that sex or lovemaking is the highest physical expression of love when individuals are expressing or sharing similar feelings. Having sex is always healthier than having wars).

Triangle Legs

Having your legs open from the knee down while standing up suggests that you may be holding back your sexuality. You may tend to demand many restrictions when it comes to sex in your relationships. Conversely, having an opening or window between you thighs while standing up may indicate that you have a strong sex drive.

Knees

Kneeling down is a way to pray, to propose, to ask for forgiveness or to communicate with a child, but the shape around your knees expresses some aspects of your personality.

Having a bump below the knee-cap suggests that you do not like to beg or ask for things from others due to your strong sense of pride or ego. In addition, you do not have the need to apologize when you make mistakes or hurt others, because you believe that others hurt themselves. However, an indentation below the knee-cap may suggest that you do not mind asking others for help.

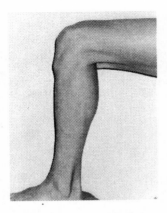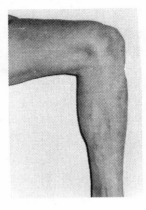

Bump below the knee   Dent below the knee

Ankles

Having skinny ankles (chicken legs) may indicate that you are sexually submissive with those whom you are intimately involved with. You always say "yes" to your loved ones because you like to please them. You are open to your partner's demands. You may encounter many sexual adventures at some point in your life if there is good chemistry between the two of you.

Wide ankles (piano legs) may indicate that you are sexually hard to get; in other words, you require great attention and demands before having sex. For example, cooking, massage, and foreplay can make you feel more emotionally and physically ready. You tend to feel that lovemaking is sacred and that your partner must earn the privilege to sleep with you.

Ankles Tilting In

Having your ankles tilting toward each other or putting more weight on the inside of your feet indicates self-centeredness and a disregard for the outside world. You usually wear off the heel of your shoes more on the inside than the outside when you dance or walk. Some physical injuries, such as hurting the outside of your feet or losing some bone can cause you to put more weight on the inside of your feet. Conversely, having your ankles leaning away from each other or putting more weight on the outside of your feet, suggests that you are inclining to the outside world and neglecting yourself. In other words, you may enjoy working more for others than for yourself. You usually wear off the heel of your shoes more on the outside than the inside when you walk or dance.

 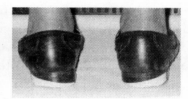

Wearing off the inside heel   Wearing off the outside heel

Feet

Your feet are indicators of the direction your thoughts are pointing to. The size and the shape of your feet can tell how you think and feel about your inner and outer worlds on and off the dance floor. The feet represent stability, balance, and connection to the earth. Healthy feet indicate an ability to handle life. However, problems with your feet may indicate that you are not grounded, or have created many obstacles in life. Typically when walking or standing still, your feet may point in different directions:

Feet Pointing Outward

Feet pointing outward may suggest that you are focusing too much on the outside world. You enjoy serving others on and off the dance floor, and you can also be affected by the outside world or people. This physical trait may also suggest that you are open to other people's positive and negative ideas. Spending more time with yourself can help you find inner wisdom, which in turn can bring you happiness. However, having your feet turned inward (pigeon-toed) suggests that you are selfish and tend to be idealistic about your personal life. This physical trait may also indicate that you are mentally closed to people's positive and negative ideas (*selfish* is when you have something and do not want to share with others, while *self-centered* is when you have something and share with others).

Feet Pointing Down

Feet pointing down while lying down indicates that you may have your mental and emotional defenses down and are having a hard time confronting others. You may experience some low self-esteem at times. Through dancing you can develop self-esteem and become more assertive. However, having your feet pointing up while lying down may suggest that you are defensive, and are emotionally and psychologically protecting yourself from others.

Tightening the toes to the ground while standing up may suggest that you are a stubborn and closed minded individual.

Arch Height

Having high arches may suggest that you are an emotional person who tends to think a lot (having your head in the clouds). You can be a dreamer and take things too personally when others hurt your emotions or feelings on and off the dance floor. In dancing you are in touch with your feelings and emotions, but at times it can be hard to control your dance movements. Learning to stay more on the ground or dragging your feet may help you to stay more grounded for more balance. Heavy padding may be needed for your dance shoes for more comfortable support of your arches.

Flat feet may suggest that you are practical, not too emotional, and realistic. You enjoy making your life simple and easy while interacting with others or with nature. You like to be emotionally detached from most people except for your loved ones. You are not a risk taker. However, if you have flat feet and have a hard time with yourself and others, it is because you are not following your nature.

Small feet may indicate that you are emotionally sensitive and afraid to take risks in life. Others can easily hurt your feelings if you are mentally fragile. You may need to work harder in order to achieve what you want. Conversely, having big feet may suggest that you are a great risk taker and great personal achiever. You may be mentally and emotionally grounded, but the outside world can easily affect you. You have ability to recover from downfalls in business and in relationships. Becoming more in touch with your emotions can bring you more inner balance.

Toes

As explained earlier, the longer your fingers are, the more easily you can grab and embrace the world. Similarly, because the lower body represents sexuality, physical endurance and practicality, the longer the toes are, the more you can experience in life:

Having spaces or windows between your long toes may suggest that you have a strong sex drive and you may experience several love affairs if you are not getting enough from one partner. You may develop sexual obsessions (when you are possessive, you become obsessive) if you are not careful. However, having no spaces or windows between your long toes may indicate that you have a strong sex drive but are sexually faithful to one partner.

Having short toes may suggest that you can attract fewer opportunities for sexual adventures. Creating more opportunities, you may experience more love affairs.

Healing physical injuries

Alternative medicine such as spiritual healing including Reiki, Polarity, Acupuncture, Massage, Chinese medicine and others can help you speed up the healing process of medical treatments on and off the dance floor. Spiritual healing helps you to release all repressed emotions, and detach the psychological trauma from your physical injuries. The following is my story of recovery from my leg injury:

> *In November 1999 I tore my entire Achilles tendon playing tennis. I did not feel any pain, but I felt the impact of someone stepping on the back of my lower leg. I had to go to the emergency room, where they put a cast on my leg. A week later, a doctor operated on my leg and gave me a boot to wear. He told me to rest and to keep my foot elevated.*
>
> *During my recovery, I received Reiki heal-*

ing, Chinese medicine, massage, and acupuncture therapy. I also kept a positive attitude regarding my leg injury, and even taught dance classes from my wheel chair. Ten weeks after my operation my doctor was very impressed when I told him that I was already doing some dancing. I attribute my unusually fast recovery to both alternative medicine and the effect a constructive mental perception had on the physical body. Therefore, by not giving a second thought to my injury, and continuing to do what I enjoyed– Reiki and teaching dancing–I helped my body naturally heal itself.

Believing in abundance allows you to share with others in need.

***

All your thoughts and emotions create your facial expressions.

***

A smile can hide your mistakes on the dance floor.

***

If you have the tendency to impress someone, it is because you want something.

***

Do not look for love, because you are love.

***

Handshakes express different messages.

***

14

Chapter 14 Self-Presentation and Personal Style

Posture and Stance

Your posture is a reflection of your mental attitude. Your perception of who you are can determine your posture as well as your health. Being aware of your posture can help you understand yourself more deeply.

Straight Posture

Straight posture indicates that you are mentally and emotionally balanced. This is another sign that you are an easygoing person with a natural ability to transcend pressure and stress from the outside world. Straight posture gives you the look of a dancer.

Slumping Posture

Slumping is often a sign of carrying too much stress, responsibilities or heavy burdens. You have been doing things for others but not enough for yourself. This causes you to become mentally and physically exhausted. This mental attitude can affect your physical body, creating pain and discomfort in your back. If you change your perception or behavior, you may release the pain and straighten your natural posture. In addition, repressing personal issues or not forgiving past relationships can cause your chest to curve in so that you develop a slight hunchback in the middle of your back. Resolving your personal issues with your loved ones may help you to release your past repressed emotions.

Upper Body Tilted Back

The tendency to naturally tilt your upper body backward may suggest that you are an emotional person. You like to make decisions with your heart or emotions. Long distance relationships may not work in the long run, because you need to see, touch and feel your partner in order to feel real. You enjoy dancing in a close position with body contact, because it gives you a sense of connection with your partner. Smooth dances such as Waltz, Foxtrot, Viennese Waltz or other slow dances can be the most comfortable for your natural posture. You are a romantic and a dreamer on and off the dance floor. Dancing with your eyes closed can be easily done, because you like to go with the flow.

Conversely, the tendency to naturally tilt your upper body forward may suggest that you are an intellectual, and analytical individual who makes decisions with your mind rather than your heart or feelings. Long distance relationships with your partner may work, because you are a sentimental and a platonic person who does not need to see, touch, and feel your partner at all times. Everything is happening in your head or mind. However, becoming in touch with your feelings can always help you to make wiser decisions on and off the dance floor. In dancing, tilting your upper body forward may give the impression that you are falling.

Upper Body tilted Backward   Upper Body tilted Forward

Raised Shoulders

Raising or lifting your shoulders may indicate that you may be inflating your ego, feeling afraid or trying to make yourself taller. In dancing, raising your shoulders may give the impression that you are tense.

Shoulders not Parallel

If you are a man who has the tendency to bring your right shoulder forward while dancing in a close position, it may suggest that you are trying to get physically and emotionally closer to your partner. However, if your partner is holding your right shoulder with her left hand while dancing in closed position, it may indicate that she is keeping her distance towards you, both emotionally and physically.

Head

This section describes how the position of your head may reveal some things about your attitude, such as leaning backward, forward, down, up, sideways, or which way you turn your head to sleep:

Head Back

Consciously or unconsciously pulling your head or face back while dancing or communicating with others may indicate that you are perceiving negative vibes, or not agreeing with what others are saying.

Head Forward

Tilting your head forward indicates that your are governed by your mind (head) rather by your feelings or heart. This also suggests that you are a visual type of person who needs to see and feel in order to believe (believing is seeing, because what you believe, sooner or later you are going to experience).

Head Down

The tendency to put your head down while walking or dancing with others may suggest that you are emotionally and mentally avoiding interaction. In dancing you may have difficulties following or leading your partner, because you are not communicating. Eye contact is crucial.

Head Up

Bringing your head or chin up while dancing or interacting with others suggests that you are feeling confident, arrogant or superior. You do not have the need to prove yourself to others because of your strong ego. Waltz, Foxtrot and Viennese Waltz are the dances that can fit your personality.

Head Tilted Sideways

Tilting your head towards your right shoulder while interacting, listening or watching others may indicate that you are experiencing some of your right-brain characteristics. On the other hand, tilting your head toward your left shoulder suggests that you are expressing some of your left-brain aspects.

Sleeping Position

Sleeping on your left side is an indication that you are expressing some of your left-brain characteristics, or perhaps you can hear more effectively with your right ear. Sleeping on your right side suggests that you are expressing some of your right-brain aspects, or you can hear more effectively with your left ear. You may tend to turn away from your partner before or while you sleep, because you need to have your own space to experience your spiritual journey, during which you often make the important decisions in your life. Sleeping on your back

JTI

may suggest that you are fearless, or confrontational with others when needed.

Arms and Hands

Arms and hands are the tools with which you express your feelings, emotions, and thoughts about someone or something:

Arms crossed

Crossed arms while interacting with others may suggest that you are emotionally unavailable or bored. Crossed arms and raising your shoulders indicates that you may be feeling cold. However, crossing your arms with your open hands on your chest may suggest that you are naturally healing or loving yourself whether you are with others or alone.

How you cross your arms can also reveal whether you are right or left brain dominant. Crossing your right arm over your left indicates that you are showing some of your left-brain dominance. Crossing your left arm over your right suggests that you are expressing some of your right-brain characteristics.

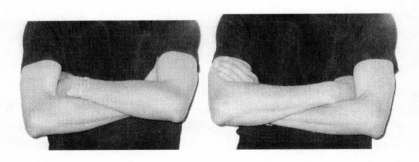

Right brain attitude   Left brain attitude

Arms Down

Having your arms down while dancing with others suggests that you are physically and emotionally passive. In dancing, you may give the impression that you are not too confident or assertive. However, taking private dance lessons for a few months can help you become more assertive and confident.

Arm Around Shoulder

Putting your arm around your partner's shoulder while walking or interacting may suggest that you are showing your warm personality or protecting your partner from intruders. This body language manifests itself when you want to let everyone know that she/he is with you.

Arm around Waist

When you put your arm around your partner's waist while dancing, standing up, or walking, it may suggest that you are mentally and emotionally submissive or allowing your partner to have the upper-hand. If the two of you put your arms around each other's waists or shoulders, it is because you think alike or have similar personalities.

Limp Arms

Having a limp right arm on and off the dance floor indicates that you may be sexually submissive to your partner. You may also be holding back some of your left-brain characteristics. However, having a limp left arm on and off the dance floor suggests that you are vulnerable to people's ideas or the outside world. You may also be repressing some of your right-brain characteristics. Generally, in dancing, if you do not offer resistance with your arms, you may not be able to follow or lead your partner. Practicing daily push-ups can help you develop strong arms and mental strength. Stiffness in your arms while dancing may suggest tension.

Arms Up

Just as boxers protect themselves by bringing their arms up to shoulder level in the ring while fighting, the same body language on the dance floor may occur when you want to protect yourself emotionally and physically. However, having your arms all the way up while dancing suggests celebration and enjoyment.

Placing Arm in front

Placing your arm in front of your partner's while holding hands may indicate that you are unconsciously or consciously showing your domineering and protective attitude. However, if your partner tends to place her/his arm behind yours, it may suggest that she/he is feeling insecure or wants physical and emotional protection.

Domineering others

Awkward Arm Movements

Feeling awkward doing graceful arm movements while dancing with your partner, may suggest that you are holding back your gentle and artistic expression. By thinking that you are tough, you cannot be gentle on the dance floor, because you think it looks feminine or silly. You worry what others think of you on the dance floor.

Blocking the Exit

Blocking the exit door with your arm or leg while interacting with others on or off the dance floor may indicate that you are craving attention or want others to listen to what you have to say. Most people want to be heard.

Creating Barriers

Holding a large or small handbag or other thing between the two of you while waking or interacting with each other may indicate that you are emotionally and mentally protecting yourself. In other words, you are placing a wall between the two of you.

Self-loved   Creating a barrier

Elbows Clamped

Dancing with your elbows clamped to your side may indicate that you are emotionally and physically protecting yourself from being hurt. However, resolving your personal issues from your past relationships can help you heal your psychological wounds. If you are learning International Latin style dance, some instructors teach you to clamp your arms on your side while dancing.

Hugging

Hugging or embracing life or people while greeting them is one of the most wonderful feelings that you can experience, but how you do it can express how you feel about yourself and others:

- A full hug with both of your arms and hands, with a soft squeeze and good intentions suggests that you have a warm personality. This is also a healing tool to relieve other people's pain.
- A hug using one arm indicates that you are emotionally and mentally halfway open. Your are holding back your feelings and keeping your distance. Learning to heal yourself first may help to heal others.
- Hugging using both hands and leaving one foot behind may also suggest that you are physically, mentally, and emotionally only somewhat open.
- Hugging others from behind may suggest that you are being protective of your loved ones. However, receiving hugs from behind indicates that you like to be emotionally and physically protected by others.
- Hugging and leaving your hands up may suggest that you are holding back emotionally.

Hands Behind your Back

The tendency to put your hands together behind your back while walking, standing up or interacting with others may suggest that you are a thinker and an intellectual individual. The Armed Forces discreetly demands that you put your hands together behind you to become psychologically and physically defenseless so you can submit to your superiors (although superiority is an illusion). Putting your hands together in front of you may suggest that you are humble and flexible to others.

Covering Face with Hand

Covering your face with your hands indicates that you are hiding yourself from shame or embarrassment over a wrong doing you have committed. You may be trying to hide emotions that you do not want to reveal through your facial expressions. For instance, if you committed a crime and got caught, you might cover your face with your hands. Conversely, if you are innocent, you may not cover your face unless you worry what others will think of you.

Covering your smile with your hand suggests that you are not fully expressing your joy to the world due to inhibition or cultural mannerism.

Scratching

Having the tendency to scratch something with your nails may suggest anger and frustration that you have built up within yourself for a long period of time. Perhaps you have not yet accepted responsibility for your own personal mistakes towards yourself and others. Being indoor too much can make things worse for you, because you are not changing environments to find other ways to release your frustrations and anger.

Unconsciously caressing your partner's hands while dancing or interacting with each other may indicate that you are needing or giving affection and love to yourself and others.

Trembling Hands

Trembling hands may indicate that you are mentally and emotionally in turmoil due to repressing your unconditional love towards yourself and others. You may have a rigid attitude about life. In dancing, shaky hands may give the impression that your are feeling nervous (people who experience Parkinson's disease may have an extreme attitude, sometimes negative, towards the outside world. They may have denied themselves and lived life for others).

Hands on your Waist

Walking with your hands on your waist with a tense look may be a sign of aggressiveness and a defensive personality. You have repressed anger and are waiting to release it by confronting others physically or verbally. Beating a pillow or screaming out loud can help you release your anger and stress.

Hands in Pockets

Putting your hands in your pockets while interacting with others suggests that you may be emotionally and physically holding back. However, putting one hand in your pocket while walking or interacting with others indicates that you are trying to look cool.

Floppy Hands

Having floppy hands or arms while dancing suggests that you are emotionally impulsive. You may be having a hard time controlling your body movements on the dance floor. Learning to control your body movements through dancing may also help you to control your emotions in the long run.

Submissive Hand

The tendency to put your hand under your partner's hand while interacting indicates that you are looking for emotional security. You may have the need to be verbally reminded by your loved ones how much they love you so you can feel good about yourself. You can only experience the love of others the way you love yourself.

Talking Hands

Talking with your hands may suggest that you are a physical, affectionate or sexual individual. You use your hands as instruments to express and communicate your feelings and emotions. In dancing, you enjoy a close dance position or body contact.

Tight Grip

Holding tight to your partner's hands while dancing can be a sign of being hard on yourself and others. You may not be feeling relaxed because you are a novice dancer. Slow dances are recommended to help you take your time. Holding tight to your partner's hands while dancing is another indication that you are having difficulty letting go when you become emotionally attached. Having your fists closed while dancing, walking or interacting with others may indicate that you are feeling tense and angry.

Open Palms

Open palms and gentle hand movements, along with a relaxed appearance while dancing or communicating with others, suggests that you are showing your tender, warm, and compassionate personality.

Clapping

Clapping is an expression of celebration for others, but the way you clap can also express your feelings towards others:

Clapping with your hands above your head while standing up or sitting down may suggest that you are open, enthusiastic, supportive, and impressed with the entertainment. Clapping at your chest level may suggest that you are open to others. Clapping with your hands down by your stomach level while sitting down or standing up may indicate that you are not being too supportive of others.

Handshake

In today's society, a handshake has become important, because it conveys certain aspects of your personality:

Giving a bland handshake (dead-fish) may suggest that you have a passive personality. You have not yet developed self-confidence in your personal life. Learning to lead more assertively while dancing can help you improve your mental strength and self-esteem.

A strong handshake with your palm down may show a possessive attitude, which in turn will lead you to obsession (possession becomes an obsession). This is another indication that you are hard on yourself and others. You like to be emotionally and physically protective of others.

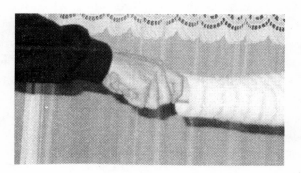

Domineering attitude

Giving a half-way closed handshake may indicate that you are emotionally and psychologically keeping your distance. You are not allowing others to become emotionally and physically close to you. You may be hiding something about yourself that you do not want to reveal. This may give the impression that you are secretive or not being honest.

Half handshake

A quick handshake indicates that you are avoiding emotional and physical interaction with others. You may feel more comfortable interacting in a one-on-one situation. A pushing-away handshake may suggest that you are keeping your distance. You may have difficulty interacting while learning or teaching dancing, because you cannot show yourself easily.

A pulling-in handshake may indicate that you need physical and emotional attention from others or are looking for love. Do not look for love because you *are* love. You have just forgotten.

An up-and-down handshake may suggest that you are an optimistic and happy individual. This also is a sign that you are happy to see the person you are greeting or shaking hands with.

Legs and Feet

Shaky Legs

Jiggling your legs to the background music while interacting and listening to others may indicate that you are distracted by the music you hear. You enjoy music and have very strong feelings for it. Jiggling your legs while sitting down or standing up may suggest that you are feeling restless and want to move around.

Bending One Leg

Bending your left leg while your partner is on your right side when you are sitting, standing up, or lying down may suggest that you are emotionally and physically protective. Your bended left leg creates a barrier to protect your partner from unwanted intruders. However, bending your right leg while your partner is on your right side suggests that you are emotionally and physically unavailable. Your leg is creating a barrier between the two of you. Bending your knees toward your chest while sitting is also another indication that you are emotionally and physically protecting yourself.

Protecting your partner   Emotionally closed   Protecting yourself

Bending Knees

Bending your knees while walking or dancing gives the impression that you are tired and suggests that you are somehow passive or holding back your assertiveness and passion for life. People may push you around emotionally. Active physical exercises such as mountain climbing, running, and doing fast dances can help you become more assertive and confident. The more you know who you are in life, the more confident you will be.

One Leg Forward

Placing one of your legs closer to someone that you are interacting with suggests that you are trying to establish physical and emotional contact. You are showing interest in invading his/her space.

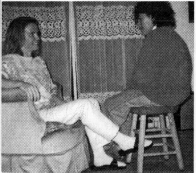

Emotionally and physically connecting with
others

Sitting with Legs Apart

You may have been taught as a young girl that it is more "ladylike" to sit with your legs together, but how you sit can reveal some aspects of your attitude:

Sitting with your legs wide open may suggest that you are a very sexual individual. It is very hard to keep your legs together for long periods of time because your body follows your mind. You may enjoy having several playmates or partners on or off the dance floor. Men show this body language more often than women, because women are taught to be sexually more discrete than men. Also, women's clothing imposes more restrictions.

Homosexuals tend to sit with their legs closed together like women do, because they enjoy expressing their feminine aspects, which make them great dancers. Lesbians may enjoy sitting with their legs wide open like men, demonstrating their masculine aspects.

Legs Apart

Walking or dancing with your legs apart may suggest that you have a strong sex drive. You may enjoy and experience different sexual affairs with different partners. You like to dance in close positions and have body contact while dancing.

Length of Stride

Taking long steps while walking or dancing may indicate that you are ambitious and have high expectations of yourself and others. Conversely, short stride or steps while dancing may suggest that you are cautious or meticulous on and off the dance floor. You may not be a risk taker, especially in your personal life, because you like to have emotional security.

Fast Walk

The tendency to walk fast may suggest that you are hyperactive, impatient, and always rushing. You may also be hard on yourself and others. Practicing smooth or slow dances with your eyes closed may help you relax and become more patient.

Floppy Steps

Flopping your feet while dancing or walking may indicate that you are having a hard time taking life or others seriously. You are projecting an "I do not care" attitude and do not like to get into other people's business, because you are emotionally and mentally disconnected. In dancing, you may give the impression that you are careless on the dance floor.

Stiff Legs

Having stiff legs while dancing suggests that you may be holding back or have a hard time relaxing with your partner sexually. This may be another sign that you have not exercised your legs enough.

On the Balls of the Feet

Dancing or walking on the balls of your feet suggests that you are an intellectual and a dreamer. You have the tendency to think a lot, and have your head in the clouds. You may be living in a world of illusions and can be superstitious (all superstitions are illusions created by you). You like to make decisions with your emotions (past experiences) rather than with your feelings, which tell you how you feel about someone in the present moment. Dancing or walking flat on your feet or wearing flat shoes may help you to become more grounded and practical. It is recommended to stay out of your mind so you can stay more in the present moment with your feelings.

Dragging your Feet

Dragging your feet while dancing or walking may indicate that you are down to earth and practical, but you are not a risk taker. However, dancing or walking with heavy steps may suggest that you are expressing anger or tension.

Putting One Foot on Top of the Other

Putting one foot on top of the other while sitting indicates that you may be hard on yourself and others. This body language is making you hold your feelings down with your foot.

Two Left Feet

Having "two left feet" (clumsy) on and off the dance floor suggests that you do not like to take instructions from others. This can make it harder to learn how to dance. If you want to learn to dance, you need to break the habit of being too rigid toward yourself and others so you begin to open your heart and be flexible to outside suggestions.

Crossed Legs

Crossing one of your legs towards your partner while sitting, standing up, or laying down indicates that you are emotionally and mentally available. However, crossing one of your legs away from your partner may suggest that you are intellectually open, but emotionally unavailable or you may be perceiving negative vibes and protecting yourself as a result. This body language is subject to change; depending on how you feel about someone or something. For example, you may be interacting with someone you like, but are feeling angry about someone else in your mind and reacting by crossing your leg over the other away from your partner.

Crossing your right leg over your left when you are alone or in front of people while sitting or lying down indicates that you may be mentally open, but emotionally closed or feeling skeptical. However, crossing your left leg over your right whether you are alone or with others suggests that your are feeling conditional. Not crossing your legs may suggest that you are feeling neutral or not showing your feelings or emotions to others.

Shaking the Hips

Shaking your hips naturally while dancing may suggest that you have a strong sex drive. You may enjoy doing Latin dances, which requires shaking your hips. Active exercises or fast dances may help you release the sexual energy that you have built up. Sticking your buttocks out while dancing may indicate that you are sexually inviting others. However, tightening your buttocks suggests that you may be sexually protecting yourself from others.

Pulling back the Pelvis

Pulling back your pelvis while dancing in a close position with a partner may demonstrate that you are sexually conservative or you are sexually protecting yourself. This body language is usually expressed more by women than men, because they are more conservative. However, pushing your pelvis forward towards your partner while dancing indicates that you have a strong sexual drive or attraction.

Facial Expression

Your facial expression can reveal how you feel about yourself and others; it is a clue to your emotions, feelings, personality, mind, and self-image. You are unconsciously and consciously communicating to everyone through your facial expressions, because all your thoughts and emotions create them.

Experimenting With Your Looks

If you are consciously making certain facial expressions to improve your looks it is because you may not be too satisfied with the one you have right now. For example, showing your upper teeth may look more appealing than showing your lower teeth. Remember that a smile always invites others to smile with you.

Angry Expression

Anger is an emotion that allows you to express your disappointment, although it should not be in a way that is violent or damaging to yourself or others. Repressing your anger can eventually cause angry facial expressions. Anger will always interfere in your present moment while you are dancing or interacting with others. It can make your dancing more aggressive, forceful, and defensive. Becoming attached to pain or anger will affect your physical body or your heart. Having a facial or a full-body massage may help you release the repressed negative emotions.

Looking Spacey

"Looking spacey" may suggest that you are distracted deep within yourself. You may be experiencing unseen images or inspiration that is coming through your mind. Great inspirations come through peace of mind. In your dancing, looking spacey may give the impression that you are not connecting with your partner.

Fearful Expression

Fear is an emotion that makes you run and hide from danger. Having a fearful expression while dancing with your partner may suggest that you are repressing your fear. Perhaps your partner is mentally, emotionally, or physically controlling you, and you are now having a hard time letting go. This fear repressed, can develop into panic attacks. In dancing, you may not be able to free yourself from your controlling partner until he/she leaves you, or changes.

If you are a novice dancer and have the tendency to not complete your steps before going into the next one, it may be a sign of your anxiety. An example would be when you are doing the basic Foxtrot step and start a new step before finishing, causing your partner confusion or to rush to keep up with you. One way to slow down and relax while you are learning is to close your eyes and focus on the step. All insecurities are illusions, so enjoy your dancing. In addition, if you tend to skip or not to finish your steps while dancing it is because you like to leave things up in the air on and off the dance floor. If you do not finish what you start it is going to pile up and become more of a burden to deal with.

Smiling

Smiling is one of the most wonderful expressions there is on and off the dance floor. It promotes self-healing and happiness. A smile can actually make you healthy at the cellular level. Smiling or laughing quietly may be a sign that you are holding back your joy. Laughing out loud may help you to become more assertive and expressive. In dancing, a smile gives the impression that you are relaxed and having a good time.

Clenching the Teeth

Clenching your teeth may be a sign that you are feeling frustrated and angry. Tense muscles around your mouth give the impression that you are ready to explode in anger due to unpleasant and unresolved past relationships. Having problems in your mouth is another indication that you are verbally repressing your emotions. Similarly, having a tight jaw demonstrates that you are repressing frustration and anger. You may be having a hard time verbally expressing your disappointments to your loved ones and others because you are afraid of being alone or rejected. In dancing, tightening the jaw or grinding your teeth may give the impression that you are mad or frustrated.

Biting the Lips

Biting your lips on and off the dance floor may suggest that you are feeling eager, sexual, angry, or are concentrating on something.

Mustache or Beard

A mustache is another physical characteristic that can reveal certain personality traits, but there are several reasons why you grow mustaches or beards:

- To hide facial scars.
- To hide emotional pain.
- To hide a gentle personality.
- To intimidate others.
- To improve your physical appearance.
- To project a macho image.
- To get attention from others.
- To save money.
- To satisfy cultural norms.
- Laziness.

Parting your Hair

Parting your hair towards your right side may suggest that you are demonstrating some of your right brain characteristics. Combing your hair to your left side indicates that you are showing some of your left-brain aspects. Parting your hair in the center suggests that you are equally showing your right and left brain dominance.

Part VI
Brain Dominance

Sticking to old habits makes it difficult to acquire new ones.

***

Love that is experiential is more powerful than words.

***

The less you fight it, the less real you make it.

***

Your present moment is your future.

***

Self-denial leads to self-destruction.

***

15

Chapter 15
Determining Your Own Brain Dominance

The purpose of this chapter is to demonstrate the differences between right and left brain characteristics in relation to your physical body. This information can give you an understanding of yourself and others, on and off the dance floor.

Right and Left-Brain Dominance

Your right brain is in control of the left side of your body while your left-brain controls your right side. Your emotions and behaviors can also manifest themselves more through your dominant side:

For example, if you stir a cup of tea with your left hand, it should naturally move clockwise in the direction of your right-brain; if you use your right hand, it will naturally move counterclockwise in the direction of your left-brain, demonstrating that you are following your natural traits. If, however, you do the opposite this suggests that you are fighting your own nature. To regain your natural dominance, practice your Latin dances by consciously moving your left arm clockwise and your right arm counterclockwise, one at a time. They are your natural movements.

Right and Left Brain Physical Indicators

You probably have asked yourself why one side of your body is longer, bigger or stronger than the other side. It is because your soul, mind and body (all three in one at the soul level) have intervened in creating the brains. If you are right brain dominant, the right-brain develops slightly faster than the left making the left side of your body slightly bigger or vice-versa. It is important to remember that you are a soul with a body and not a body with a soul, because it is the soul that gives life to your physical body (the soul carries the body).

Right-Brain Physical Indicators:

- Active left side of the body.
- Birthmarks on the left side of the body.
- Dimple on the left cheek.
- Healthy left side of the body.
- Hair growing faster on the left side of the head.
- Longer, heavier and stronger left side of the body.
- More milk is produced in your left breast.
- Sensitive left side of the body.
- Stronger hearing in the left ear.
- Stronger vision in the left eye.
- Very little hair on the body.
- Warm temperature body.

Left-brain Physical Indicators:

- Active right side of the body.
- Birthmarks on the right side of the body.
- Cold temperature body.
- Dimple on the right cheek.
- Healthy right side of the body.
- Hair growing faster on the right side of the head.
- Longer, heavier and stronger right side of the body.
- More milk is produced in your right breast.
- Sensitive right side of the body.
- Stronger hearing in the right ear.
- Stronger vision in the right eye.

Unnatural Dominance

It is possible that you have been born right-brain dominant and become left-brain oriented or vice-versa because of your society and your family value system. This creates conflicts between yourself and your own nature, because you do not know whom or what to follow.

Right-Brain Characteristics

The following are your right-brain personal characteristics:

- You are assertive and like to be yourself.
- You like to express your feelings through actions rather than words or promises.
- You are artistic and original, and do not like to copy other people's ideas.
- You can be adaptable to others or to different environments.

- You are a believer and open-minded to the unknown, but sometimes too gullible.
- You like tangible or close relationships rather than distant ones.
- You like contemplating life or people's nature.
- You are creative, resourceful, and enjoy putting your ideas into practical use.
- You are colorful, humorous, and enjoy wearing a great variety of vivid colors.
- You are a conformist and easy to satisfy.
- You do not follow outside instructions most of the time, but your own.
- You can be easily distracted by the outside world or others.
- You are easy and gentle on yourself and others, and do not believe in suffering.
- You can be emotionally strong, but detached from others, because you do not feel responsible for their happiness or unhappiness.
- If you are a man, you have some feminine body features, or body language, which help you relate more comfortably to women.
- You have a flexible personality, because you are easy-going on yourself and others.
- You are forgiving toward yourself and others, because you do not take things too personally.
- You are a free spirit and do not need a role model in life. You are able to emotionally handle separation or divorce from your loved ones.
- You are a natural leader and do not like to follow others when it comes to your personal goals.
- You are healthy, a big eater, and positive about life.
- You are at peace with yourself, sleep well and do not worry much.
- You are a feeling or heart thinker, and a humanitarian.

- You are aware of your inner world, which makes you more spiritually aware of life.
- You are intuitive and believe that there are no accidents or coincidences in life, nor victims or villains, because you are the creator of your own life.
- You can be lazy and like to take your time in doing things, because you do not believe in working too hard.
- You live in the moment and do not worry about the past or the future.
- You are mentally strong, grounded, realistic, and practical about life.
- You believe that there is always enough of everything for everybody.
- You are natural because you are not trying to be anyone else but yourself.
- You do not need recognition from others because you know and appreciate yourself.
- You are not a complainer because you accept yourself and others for who they are.
- You are not controlling of others because you love others unconditionally.
- You do not have great expectations of yourself or of others, because you are not attached to results but rather to creation.
- You are not an extremist because you like to be balanced.
- You are not goal oriented because you like to go in many different directions.
- You are not meticulous, prejudiced or picky because you do not have preferences, is only experiences.
- You are not a perfectionists because you do not like little details.
- You are not a reader because you prefer to listen to your inner voice or wisdom.
- You are romantic through your own actions or dancing.

- You are not vengeful toward anyone because you believe in natural consequences and outcomes of every individual act. You do not believe in punishment.
- You are optimistic because you always find solutions for everything.
- You like to be outdoors because you do not like to be caged in.
- You are generally patient or tolerant because you understand yourself and others.
- You are physical, sexual, healthy, and affectionate toward others (being sexual or being affectionate depends on your intentions).
- You have a short memory, which helps you to forget and forgive what others have done to you.
- You like simplicity in order to make things more practical.
- You are social and like the company of others.
- You are spontaneous in your actions because you like to listen to your feelings.
- You are spiritual and interested in the metaphysical aspects of life.
- You trust others because you do not have to. However, you cannot trust those who you do not know.
- You give unconditional love to yourself and others because love is unlimited.
- You are not aggressive or violent, because you do not let your anger build up.

Left-Brain Dominance

The following are your left-brain personal characteristics:

- You like to express your feelings through words, promises, and sometimes through actions.
- You are not naturally too artistic, but like to copy or be inspired by other people's ideas.
- You may have a hard time adapting to most environments.
- You are a non-believer, skeptical, and are not gullible.
- You are sentimental, platonic, and may enjoy distant relationships.
- You like to know about other people's lives more than your own.
- You can be creative or resourceful based on your intellectuality or past experiences.
- You like to wear conservative colors such as blue, black, brown and white.
- You are a non-conformist and hard to satisfy.
- You feel more comfortable following outside instructions and doing things for other people.
- You like to be focused, and not be distracted by the outside world or others.
- You are hard on yourself and others, and like to achieve things the hard way in order to be appreciated.
- You are an introvert and do not like revealing yourself to others.
- You believe that there is not enough of everything for everybody so you cannot share much.
- You can be emotionally attached to others and feel responsible for other people's happiness or unhappiness.
- If you are a woman, you may have more masculine body features, or body language, which help you relate more comfortably to men.
- You may have an inflexible personality, because you do not like to adapt to others.

- You do not easily forgive yourself or others because you take things personally and have strong attachment to guilt.
- You are not too grounded, realistic, or practical about life.
- You think that you are not a free spirit and need a role model to feel good about yourself. It can be hard to handle separation or divorce from your loved ones.
- You can be a leader through hard work and make everybody work hard as well.
- You can be unhealthy at times, and you are not a big eater.
- You are not at peace with yourself, sleep little, and worry a lot about others.
- You make decisions based on your mind or head rather than your feelings or heart.
- You are not too aware of your inner world, which makes you less spiritual, but more materialistic.
- You believe in accidents, coincidences, victims, and villains, because that is the way you learned to be.
- You do not like to take your time about things or dare to be lazy because you are impatient.
- You like to live your life in the past to remember who you were and live in the future to be someone else.
- You are trying to be someone else because you do not know who you really are. You create yourself out of the experience of others.
- You need recognition from others because you do not appreciate yourself enough.
- You are a complainer because you are not too satisfied with yourself and others.
- You can be controlling toward your loved ones and others because you are not accepting them for who they are.

- You have great expectations of yourself and others, because you are attached to results, which in turn become disappointments.
- You are an extremist because you like to push yourself.
- You are goal oriented because you like to go in one direction.
- You are meticulous, prejudiced, and picky because you have preferences. You are a perfectionist because you like little details.
- You are an intellectual and like to read a lot because you want to know about many things.
- You are romantic and a dreamer.
- You can be vengeful because you have kept your anger as a self-defense mechanism. You believe in punishment.
- You are pessimistic and skeptical, which make it harder to find solutions for everything.
- You like to be indoors because you like to be in your own intellectual world.
- You are impatient and intolerant because you do not understand yourself or others.
- You are not too affectionate, but like to express yourself through words.
- You have a great memory, which helps you not to forget and forgive what others have done to you.
- You like to put forth strong effort to achieve what you need.
- You are not too spontaneous in your actions because you like to plan ahead for less disappointments.
- You believe in science so you can prove to yourself or to others what you believe (believing is seeing rather than seeing is believing because what you believe you are going to experience).

- You do not trust yourself or others, because you do not love yourself or others enough.
- You give conditional love because you believe that love is limited. You are a loner.
- You can be aggressive or violent because you have repressed your anger. You tend to react to the outside world.

Healing the Mind, Healing the Body

Living in this left-brained dominant, primitive, and spiritually limited society, you have grown up with many restrictions, strong value system, and created yourself out the experience of others. As a result, you have been repressing your emotions and your feelings, creating all the problems in your physical and mental body. In order to heal your body, you must first heal your mind, since your mind has been responsible for creating all your mental and physical problems in life. The following are ways to change your perception about yourself, which in turn will heal your body:

- Remember that you are not here in this life to learn anything, but to remember who you are (your soul already knows everything).
- Remember to love yourself first before loving another.
- Remember to help yourself first before helping another.
- Remember to understand yourself first before understanding another.
- Remember to know your body first before knowing another.
- Remember to give to yourself first before giving to another.
- Remember to express all your emotions without damaging yourself or another.

- Remember not to judge nor condemn yourself or another, just observe.
- Remember to understand your own body language first before understanding another's.
- Remember to be joy because your soul is joy.

Family Tree and Brain Dominance

The following characterizes the impact of birth order on brain dominance:

It is important to know and remember that you are three beings in one (body, mind, spirit) at the energy level. In other words, your DNA already existed at your soul or energy level, before coming to your physical body. Therefore, you do not inherit your parents' personalities *you just borrow some physical traits of your parents before birth,* because you are coming through them and not from them. The law of attraction in the Universe may help you understand that like attracts like. In other words, similarities attract. Even if you have been adopted as a child you are attracting the experience of having these particular parents.

If you are a first or third-born child, you are left-brain dominant and have more your father's personality than your mother's. However, if you consider yourself more like your mother than your father, it is because you may have spent more time with your mother. In turn this may create some conflicts in your personality, because you may be repressing your natural identity similar to your father's.

If you are a second or fourth born child, you are right-brain dominant and have more your mother's personality than your father's. However, if you consider yourself to have more your father's personality it is because you may have spent more time with him. In turn this may create some conflict in your personality because you may be repressing your natural identity similar to your mother's.

If you are a first-born twin, you are left-brain dominant (father's personality). However, if you have one older brother or sister you are right-brain dominant or the second-born child. If you are a second born twin, you are right-brain dominant (mother's personality).

No Apparent Dominance

If you have no visible difference in length between the right and left side of your body, you are balanced. This means not only that you are more balanced than those who are just more right or more left-brain dominant, but also that you have the potential to balance both sides of your brain.

Dominance Quiz

The following are typical characteristics of the right and left-brain person, although this does not mean that you are your brains. You are a soul, which holds your physical body.

If you are a right or left-brain dominant person and find yourself unhappy, perhaps this is a sign that you may need to change or follow more of your left or right-brain characteristics in order to bring harmony into your inner world.

To determine whether you are more right or left-brain dominant, highlight the following personality traits that apply to you:

Right Brain Characteristics   Left Brain Characteristics

Right Brain Characteristics	Left Brain Characteristics
Assertive	Shy
Action oriented	Verbal
Ambidextrous	Some Ambidextrous
Artistic	Linguistic
Adaptable	Not adaptable
Believer	Nonbeliever
Bright Colors	Earth colors
Close relationship	Long distant relationship
Contemplative	Reactive
Creative	Rational
Conformist	Nonconformist
Content	Discontent
Dislikes structure	Needs structure
Distracted	Focused
Easy on self	Hard on self
Introverted	Extroverted
Emotionally strong	Emotionally vulnerable
Feminine aspect	Masculine aspect
Flexible	Inflexible
Forgiving	Difficult to forgive
Free spirit	Analytical
Goes with the flow	Goes against the flow
Healthy	Healthy off and on
Heavy sleeper	Light sleeper
Heart thinker	Head thinker
Humorous	Serious
Into themselves	Into others
Knowing enough	Wants to know everything
Lazy thinker	Excessive thinker
Lives in the moment	Lives in the past and future
Mentally strong	Mentally fragile
Mind not too crowded	Crowded mind

Needs little attention	Needs great attention
Not a complainer	Complainer
Not domineering	Domineering
No expectations	Expectations
Not extremist	Extremist
Not goal oriented	Goal oriented
Nonjudgmental	Judgmental
Not meticulous	Meticulous
Not a perfectionist	Perfectionist
Non reader	Reader
Not romantic	Romantic
Not vengeful	Vengeful
Not routine	Routine
Not too rancorous	Rancorous
Not rule-bound	Rule-bound
Non sequential	Sequential
Non sentimental	Sentimental
Open-minded	Closed-minded
Optimistic	Pessimistic
Not too organized	Organized
Original	Imitator
Passive	Persistent
Patient	Impatient
Physical	Intellectual
Practical	Dreamer
No need of role model	Needs role model
Short memory	Strong memory
Simple	Complex
Somewhat emotional	Emotional
Social	Loner
Spontaneous	Planner
Spiritual	Materialistic
Tolerant	Not too tolerant
Trusting	Mistrustful
Verbally not too communicative	Verbally very communicative

| Unconventional | Conventional |
| Unconditional | Conditional |

PART VII
APPENDIX

You are not here to learn anything,
only to remember and experience what your soul
already knows.
***

Life is meaningless until you put meaning into it.
***

You cannot judge nor condemn, only observe.
***

Nothing is real in life except your spirit.
***

Ignorance produces tragedy.
***

Appendix Origins of Some Ballroom Dances

Many of you may not know the history of ballroom dancing, because dance studios may not offer enough information about it. However, instructors should take time on their own to find out more about ballroom dance in the libraries. Here is some basic information:

- Foxtrot came from the US in the 1950s.
- Hustle came from France in the 1970s.
- Mambo, Cha-cha & Rumba came from Cuba in the 1940s.
- Merengue came from the Dominican Republic in the 1950s.
- Paso Doble came from Spain in the 1920s.
- Polka came from Germany in the 1950s.
- Rock-and-roll came from the US in the 1940s.
- Samba came from Brazil in the 1920s.
- Salsa came from Puerto Rico in the 1960s.
- Swing & Jitterbug came from the U.S in the 1930s.
- Tango came from Spain, France and Italy in the 1800s.
- Viennese Waltz came from Vienna, Austria in the 1800s.

All dance steps and turns can be used the same way for many different dances in different tempos. For example, all hustle turns can be used in Merengue. All dances borrow steps from each other.

In addition, in the last decade, in the video music industry, more and more dances from around the world are becoming popular in today's society to help dancers create new forms of movements and to get in touch with their spirits. All these dances can expand dancers' horizons to further understand others from a cultural or psychological point of view.

*Thought is energy, energy is sound, sound is color,
color is music, music is movement, movement is
expression, expression is feeling and feeling is love,
the language of the soul.*
***

*If you do not know where you are going after here,
you may be afraid of going there.*
***

The body draws movements through music.
***

*We are all from heaven and
we always come back to heaven.*
***

Music heals the body.
***

Appendix B Music for Dancing

Music brings all civilizations together, because a note or a word in a hundred different languages expresses the same feeling, thought, idea or intention. Music affects your soul, mind and body, and it can bring back memories of happiness, pain or sadness. Music can heal the mind and therefore the body. Whether you have any dance background or not, music draws out your body movements and triggers joy.

Music is a universal language that has many personalities, feelings, and expresses many histories. For example, slow music brings out togetherness, sensuality, introspection, relaxation, sadness, and romanticism. Fast music brings out joy, celebration, energy, passion, playfulness, pain, flirtation, tragedy, love and happiness.

Types of Music

International

Dancing or listening to international or foreign music suggests that you are connected and open to different cultures. Foreign music or songs possess no barriers to prevent you from enjoying yourself, since even if you cannot understand the words, you can feel the message.

Heavy Metal

The tendency to listen or dance to loud heavy metal music suggests that you may be in pain. This kind of music triggers unhappiness that is repressed within you, and the more pain you have, the more violent you may become. The loudness of this music can damage your hearing and be stressful.

Mellow Music

Listening to mellow music such as classical, jazz or meditation music may suggest that you are a relaxed and content person. You may also unconsciously like to listen to this music, because you are a hyperactive individual or need to relax from your hectic environment. However, if you do not like slow music, it is because you like to keep active.

Blues

The tendency to listen or dance to blues music may suggest that you are experiencing pain and sadness. West Coast swing, Rumbas, and Argentine Tango music may trigger your pain and sadness.

Love Songs

Listening to romantic music may suggest that you are a sentimental individual who likes to be in love or in pain. You like to remember your past relationships. When someone breaks your heart (because you allow it) then, you start attracting love songs wherever you are. This is another sign that you have not yet let go of your past relationships. However, love or sexy songs can also turn couples on when dancing close together.

Healing Music

Healing music are sounds of energy that can help you relieve your discomfort within yourself. This subliminal music touches your soul, and your heart, which heals your pain or sadness. Some hospitals use relaxing music to reduce the amount of tranquilizers given to patients before surgery. Healing music or subliminal songs (message to the subconscious) can heal the energies of your illness or sickness by its curative sounds. When you become consciously aware of this tool, you can use it.

Nature Music

The tendency to listen to nature music or sounds such the rain, the ocean, the wind, the birds, thunder, and crackling fire means that you are in touch and concerned with your surroundings. This music can bring inspiration to your dance choreographies at social events and dance competitions.

Variety of Music

Listening to all kinds of music may suggest that you are a flexible individual who enjoys different life styles and people. The greater the variety of music you listen to, the more flexible you can be in expressing yourself through dancing.

Feeling the music

Music is a feeling not a concept or a word. Therefore, it is important that you be out of your mind for a few minutes so you can become more in touch with your soul, mind, body, and music. Sit in a quiet place with your eyes closed and listen to a particular piece of music you like, and allow your body and soul to respond naturally. If your body or soul does not respond you may not be ready yet. However, if you do this every day for a few minutes, you will eventually begin to feel the music. Do not eat, chew gum or distract yourself with anything, because it may take longer to feel the music.

Lyrics and Their Impact

Many songs are written to remind you of your insecurities and problems in life, because the same lyrics you hear over and over become implanted in your mind (brain-washing). For example, when you hear songs such as the following and identify with the lyrics, you are adopting the attitudes in the song. These lyrics only validate your insecurities and doubts about who you are, leading you into more ignorance and therefore more suffering:

- "I cannot live without you," makes you feel worthless.
- "I am nothing without you," makes you lack self identity.
- "You belong to me," makes you possessive and obsessive.
- "I belong to you," makes you depend on others.
- "Burn in hell," makes you condemn your loved ones and your enemies.
- "I cannot let go of you," makes you feel trapped.
- "You are everything to me," makes you neglect others.
- "God will punish you if you are not good to him," makes you fear God.

Constructive Music

Constructive or healing music can send a different message to you and the world so you can improve yourself and regain your happiness:

- "If you leave me, I understand," means I love you uncon-
ditionally.
- "We are all one," means that all spirits are one and equal.
- "Evil does not exist," means do not worry about punish-
ment.
- "I see your true colors," means you are yourself.
- "Likes attracts like," means we are similar.
- "Only when you know what love is, can you experience
it," means when you know something you can experi-
ence it.
- "Death does not exist," means we always comeback to
play a different game.
- "I don't need to look for love," means I am love.
- "Let me rock your world baby," means I want to have
fun with you.
- "Hell does not exist," means there is only heaven, here
and hereafter.
- "What you give to yourself, give to others," means we
are all one.

Final Word

The standard left and right brain negative aspects may no longer apply to you. In other words, you may have evolved spiritually and you are now living your life freely without restrictions, judgments, expectations, or preferences. You have mastered your life and become aware that there is no right or wrong, only love. You have become love or your feelings. When people see themselves though you, they will want to evolve around you until they become like you. We are all going in different directions looking for the same thing—*to be one with everyone and everything*. This journey never ends, because the more evolved you become, the more there is to know.

Studying the body language of dance, the body features, and the right and left brain characteristics were, are, and always will be an incredible spiritual journey for me. It has helped me to understand, and improve my communication skills and my relationships with myself and others. It has especially enabled me to express my joy more fully. You too may already be experiencing this wonderful journey. I hope this book will bring you a deeper awareness of yourself on and off the dance floor.